WORLD IN CONFLICT

SOUTH AFRICA
NATION IN TRANSITION

SOUTH AFRICA
NATION IN TRANSITION

by Peter Kizilos

Lerner Publications Company / Minneapolis

Website address: www.lernerbooks.com

All maps by Philip Schwartzberg, Meridian Mapping, Minneapolis.
Cover photo by Archive Photos/Juda Ngwenya/Reuters.
Table of contents photos (from top to bottom) by South African Tourism Board; Independent Picture Service; *Illustrated London Times;* CICR/Luc Chessex; photo courtesy of the Peace Corps.

Series Consultant: Andrew Bell-Fialkoff
Editor: Kari Cornell
Editorial Director: Mary M. Rodgers
Designer: Michael Tacheny
Photo Researcher: Cheryl Hulting

LIBRARY OF CONGRESS CATALOGING-IN-PUBLICATION DATA

Kizilos, Peter.
    South Africa: nation in transition/ by Peter Kizilos
      p.   cm.—(World in conflict series)
    Includes bibliographical references and index.
    Summary: A historical account of the ethnic conflict in this land of contrasts; includes a discussion of current issues and challenges.
    ISBN 0–8225–3558–0 (lib. bdg. : alk. paper)
    1. South Africa—Politics and government—20th century—Juvenile literature. 2. South Africa—Race relations. 3. South Africa—Ethnic relations—Juvenile literature. [1. South Africa—Politics and government. 2. South Africa—race relations.] I. Title. II. Series: World in conflict.
DT1924.K59 1998
305.8'00968—DC21   97–6774

Manufactured in the United States of America
1 2 3 4 5 6 – JR – 03 02 01 00 99 98

CONTENTS

ABOUT THIS SERIES

Government firepower kills 25 protesters . . . Thousands of refugees flee the country . . . Rebels attack capital . . . Racism and rage flare . . . Fighting breaks out . . . Peace talks stall . . . Bombing toll rises to 52 . . . Slaughter has cost up to 50,000 lives.

Conflicts between people occur across the globe, and we hear about some of the more spectacular and horrific episodes in the news. But since most fighting doesn't directly affect us, we often choose to ignore it. And even if we do take the time to learn about these conflicts—from newspapers, magazines, television news, or radio—we're often left with just a snapshot of the conflict instead of the whole reel of film.

Most news accounts don't tell you the whole story about a conflict, focusing instead on the attention-grabbing events that make the headlines. In addition, news sources may have a preconceived idea about who is right and who is wrong in a conflict. The stories that result often portray one side as the "bad guys" and the other as the "good guys."

The *World in Conflict* series approaches each conflict with the idea that wars and political disputes aren't simply about bullies and victims. Conflicts are complex problems that can often be traced back hundreds of years. The people fighting one another have complicated reasons for doing so. Fighting erupts between groups divided by ethnicity, religion, and nationalism. These groups fight over power, money, territory, control. Sometimes people who just want to go about their own business get caught up in a conflict just because they're there.

These books examine major conflicts around the world, some of which are very bloody and others that haven't involved a lot of violence. They portray the people involved in and affected by conflicts. They describe how each conflict got started, how it developed, and where it stands. The books also outline some of the ways people have tried to end the conflicts. By reading the stories behind the headlines, you will learn some reasons why people hate and fight one another and, in addition, why some people struggle so hard to end conflicts.

WORDS YOU NEED TO KNOW

Afrikaner: White immigrants to South Africa who speak Afrikaans, a language derived from Dutch. The early Afrikaners were white settlers who came to South Africa from Holland, Germany, and France.

amnesty: Pardon granted by a government or other authority to a person or group found guilty of committing politically motivated crimes. The Truth and Reconciliation Commission had the power to grant amnesty to those who applied.

Boer: A Dutch word meaning "farmer." It is also used to refer to Afrikaner farmers. See above description.

coalition: An association, grouping, or compact formed between the representatives of different interest groups or political parties. The ANC, the National Party, and the Inkatha Freedom Party formed a coalition government.

consensus: Making decisions by reaching an agreement of all those concerned. For the first two years after Nelson Mandela was elected president of South Africa, the Government of National Unity made virtually all decisions by consensus.

economic sanctions: Restrictions, restraints, or embargoes that prohibit or limit trade or diplomatic relations between countries. During apartheid, many nations, including the United States, passed diplomatic and economic sanctions against South Africa.

ethnic group: A permanent group of people bound together by a combination of cultural markers, which may include—but are not limited to—race, nationality, tribe, religion, customs, and historical origins.

guerrilla tactics: A method of fighting that is radical, aggressive, or unconventional. It is often used by rebel fighters who are not associated with an internationally recognized government security force.

militia group: A supplementary fighting force. Often but not always, this term is used to describe underground, illegal groups. Sometimes an illegal militia group may support, through the use of violence, the current government and its policies. The aim of other militia groups is the overthrow of the government.

state of emergency: A situation in which the government suspends civil liberties such as freedom of speech, association, or religion in order to deal with a perceived threat to its survival. During apartheid, South Africa's white government often declared a state of emergency to clamp down on protesters.

vigilante: a member of a volunteer committee organized to suppress and punish crime when the processes of law seem inadequate.

white supremacist group: A group of conservative whites who believe that white people are superior to nonwhites and people of other races. The largest organized group of white supremacists in South Africa is the Afrikaner Resistance Movement (AWB).

FOREWORD

by Andrew Bell-Fialkoff

Conflicts between various groups are as old as time. Peoples and tribes around the world have fought one another for thousands of years. In fact our history is in great part a succession of wars—between the Greeks and the Persians, the English and the French, the Russians and the Poles, and many others. Not only do states or ethnic groups fight one another, so do followers of different religions—Catholics and Protestants in Northern Ireland, Christians and Muslims in Bosnia, and Buddhists and Hindus in Sri Lanka. Often ethnicity, language, and religion—some of the main distinguishing elements of culture—reinforce one another in characterizing a particular group. For instance, the vast majority of Greeks are Orthodox Christian and speak Greek; most Italians are Roman Catholic and speak Italian. Elsewhere, one cultural aspect predominates. Serbs and Croats speak dialects of the same language but remain separate from one another because most Croats are Catholics and most Serbs are Orthodox Christians. To those two groups, religion is more important than language in defining culture.

We have witnessed an increasing number of conflicts in modern times—why? Three reasons stand out. One is that large empires—such as Austria-Hungary, Ottoman Turkey, several colonial empires with vast holdings in Asia, Africa, and America, and, most recently, the Soviet Union—have collapsed. A look at world maps from 1900, 1950, and 1998 reveals an ever-increasing number of small and medium-sized states. While empires existed, their rulers suppressed many ethnic and religious conflicts. Empires imposed order, and local resentments were mostly directed at the central authority. Inside the borders of empires, populations were multiethnic and often highly mixed. When the empires fell apart, world leaders found it impossible to establish political frontiers that coincided with ethnic boundaries. Different groups often claimed territories inhabited by others. The nations created on the lands of a toppled empire were saddled with acute border and ethnic problems from their very beginnings.

The second reason for more conflicts in modern times stems from the twin ideals of freedom and equality. In the United States, we usually think of freedom as "individual freedom." If we all have equal rights, we are free. But if you are a member of a minority group and feel that you are being discriminated against, your group's rights and freedoms are also important to you. In fact, if you don't have your "group freedom," you don't have full individual freedom either.

After World War I (1914–1918), the allied western nations, under the guidance of U.S. President Woodrow Wilson, tried to satisfy group rights by promoting minority rights. The spread of frantic nationalism in the 1930s, especially among disaffected ethnic minorities, and the catastrophe of World War II (1939–1945) led to a fundamental reassessment of the Wilsonian philosophy. After 1945 group rights were downplayed on the assumption that guaranteeing individual rights would be sufficient. In later decades, the collapse of multiethnic nations like Czechoslovakia, Yugoslavia, and the Soviet Union—coupled with the spread of nationalism in those regions—came as a shock to world leaders. People want democracy and individual rights, but they want their group rights, too. In practice, this means more conflicts and a cycle of secession, as minority ethnic groups seek their own sovereignty and independence.

The fires of conflict are often further stoked by the media, which lavishes glory and attention on independence movements. To fight for freedom is an honor. For every Palestinian who has killed an Israeli, there are hundreds of Kashmiris, Tamils, and Bosnians eager to shoot at their enemies. Newspapers, television and radio news broadcasts, and other media play a vital part in fomenting that sense of honor. They magnify each crisis, glorify rebellion, and help to feed the fire of conflict.

The third factor behind increasing conflict in the world is the social and geographic mobility that modern society enjoys. We can move anywhere we want and can aspire—or so we believe—to be anything we wish. Every day the television tantalizingly dangles the prizes that life can offer. We all want our share. But increased mobility and ambition also mean increased competition, which leads to antagonism. Antagonism often fastens itself to ethnic, racial, or religious differences. If you are an inner-city African American and your local grocer happens to be Korean American, you may see that individual as different from yourself—an intruder—rather than as a person, a neighbor, or a grocer. This same feeling of "us" versus "them" has been part of many an ethnic conflict around the world.

Many conflicts have been contained—even solved—by wise, responsible leadership. But unfortunately, many politicians use citizens' discontent for their own ends. They incite hatred, manipulate voters, and mobilize people against their neighbors. The worst things happen when neighbor turns against neighbor. In Bosnia, in Rwanda, in Lebanon, and in countless other places, people who had lived and worked together and had even intermarried went on a rampage, killing, raping, and robbing one another with gusto. If the appalling carnage teaches us anything, it is that we should stop seeing one another as hostile competitors and enemies and accept one another as people. Most importantly, we should learn to understand why conflicts happen and how they can be prevented. That is why *World in Conflict* is so important—the books in this series will help you understand the history and inner dynamics of some of the most persistent conflicts of modern times. And understanding is the first step to prevention. ⊕

INTRODUCTION

An aerial view of South Africa reveals striking topographical contrasts. Lush green valleys fold into majestic mountain ranges, and rainy subtropical coastal regions dwindle to hot, dry deserts.

A deeper look at South Africa shows that the lifestyles of the people are as varied as the land in which they live. A small number of South Africans live in a wealthy nation filled with shining cities and sprawling suburbs. These citizens enjoy a standard of living equal to that of the United States, Canada, and western European countries. These South Africans, most of whom are white, work in large cities, drive new cars, and send their children to good schools.

The majority of South Africans, however, live quite differently. Far from a developed nation, their land more closely resembles an impoverished country. The people in this South Africa are poor, uneducated, and live in run-down shacks with no electricity or running water. Those lucky enough to have jobs must travel long distances by bus or train to get from their homes to the cities where they work. Most people living in this South Africa are black, Coloured, or Asian.

For more than 40 years—from 1948 to 1990—South Africans lived under a system of apartheid—an **Afrikaner** word meaning "separateness" or "apartness." Under apartheid South Africa's white minority continued the pattern of domination over the country's nonwhite majority that it had started nearly a century earlier. The laws that ruling whites passed systematically deprived nonwhites of land, property, freedoms, educational and career opportunities, and self-respect.

To rebel against the laws, many blacks joined political action groups like the African National Congress (ANC), a civil rights organization formed in 1912 to promote

Drawing the boundaries for South Africa's nine provinces was a complex and difficult task. Negotiators had to balance the principle of majority rule with the desire to protect the rights of South Africa's diverse minorities. As of 1994, South Africa's homelands ceased to exist, and nonwhites were free to live anywhere in the country.

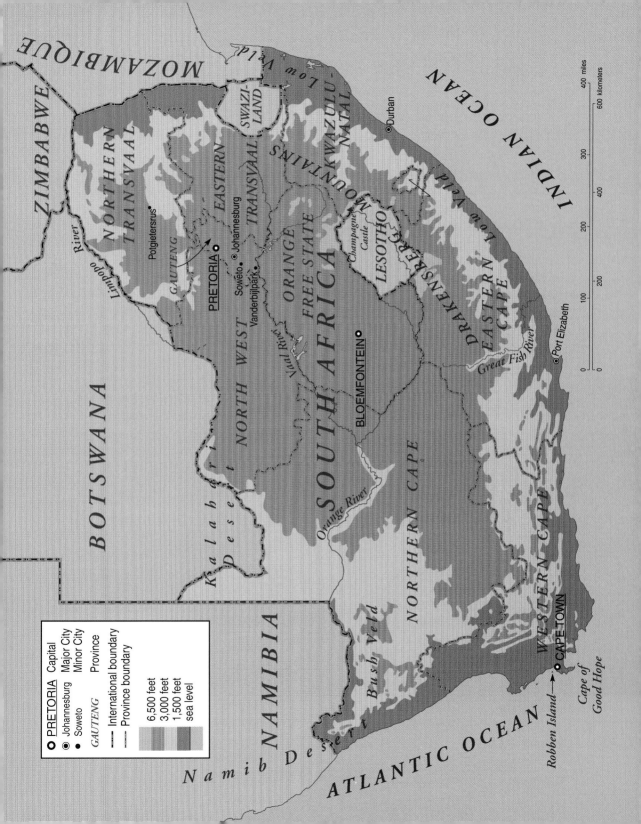

the interests of black South Africans. At first the ANC staged peaceful protests to counter apartheid laws. But when South African police killed 69 black protesters in 1960, the ANC turned to violence and terrorism. The government fought back. Apartheid leaders outlawed the ANC and other political groups, used force to break up protests, and imprisoned, beat, and sometimes murdered political activists. The conflict escalated into a near war lasting more than 30 years, in which thousands of people were injured or killed. Apartheid has been dismantled, and these days South Africa is ruled by an ANC-led democratic government that strives to respect the rights of all people. Yet the old system left a legacy of inequality, mistrust, and unrest.

THE LAND

South Africa is bordered by the Indian Ocean on the east, the Atlantic Ocean on the west, and the nations of Namibia, Botswana, Zimbabwe, Mozambique, and Swaziland on the north. The Indian and Atlantic Oceans meet at the Cape of Good Hope, a narrow point jutting out from the southwestern coast. In the eastern part of the country, South Africa's borders surround the independent, mountainous country of Lesotho.

Covering an area of about 472,000 square miles, South Africa is about twice the size of Texas. Most of South Africa's interior is a plateau, a flat area raised significantly above the land that surrounds it. The Great Escarpment, a wall of mountain ranges, divides inland plateaus from coastal lowlands in the southeast. Elevations range from sea level along the coast to more than 11,000 feet at Champagne Castle, the highest peak in the Drakensberg mountain range on Lesotho's southern border. The Kalahari Desert stretches across parts of northwestern South Africa

Rivers crash down the plateaus of South Africa's rugged landscape to create many waterfalls. This one is in Johannesburg.

Minneapolis Public Library and Information Center

SOUTH AFRICA *Nation in Transition*

and extends northward into Botswana and Namibia, and the Namib Desert lies along the western coast and also reaches into Namibia. Three major rivers—the Orange, the Vaal, and the Limpopo—wind their way through the South African landscape.

Most of South Africa has a mild, temperate climate. Vegetation found in South Africa varies depending on the regional rainfall levels. In general more rain falls in the eastern part of the country and along the southern coast, where subtropical rain forests grow. Prairies and grasslands cover the drier central part of the country. In areas where rainfall is especially slight—also called the veld in South Africa—coarse desert grasses, scattered trees, and shrubs are the only plants that thrive.

PROVINCES AND CITIES

South Africa is the richest, most populous, and most urban nation in southern Africa. In 1996 about 46 million people lived in South Africa. The population has steadily grown over the past several decades. About half of all South Africans live in and around the country's

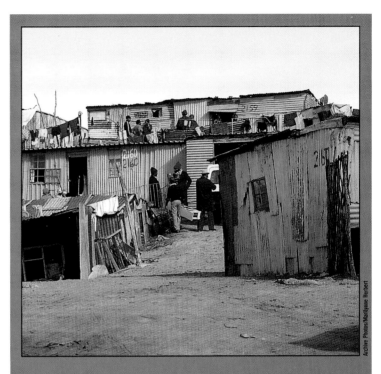

During apartheid the government established homelands in the dry, barren bush veld, low veld, and Kalahari Desert—the least productive areas of the country—and moved blacks into these resettlement camps. It was nearly impossible to grow crops in the camps, which had no running water, electricity, or other resources. Various apartheid laws enabled the government to push 73 percent of the population onto 13 percent of the land area. From 1960 to 1986 alone, more than 3.5 million blacks were forcibly moved from white-designated areas to black areas.

Overcrowding in the homelands was a major problem. As a result, black townships sprang up on the outskirts of white cities, towns, and suburbs. Yet the townships were also overcrowded. Large extended families lived in cramped one- or two-room shacks. While the homes of prosperous whites had high gates and swimming pools, black homes like those shown here in Crossroads, a Cape Town township, had no running water or electricity.

The 32 languages and dialects spoken in South Africa reflect the country's diversity. English and Afrikaans, the languages featured on this sign, were once the only two official languages. In 1994, that number grew to 12 to also include Zulu, Xhosa, Sotho, Tswana, Dutch, Portuguese, Italian, Chinese, Hindi, and Greek. Most South Africans are bilingual, and many can speak three or four languages.

Archive Photos/Camera Press

major metropolitan areas such as Cape Town (population 1.9 million), Johannesburg (population 4 million), Durban (population 982,075), and Pretoria (population 822,925). The rest of the population lives in small towns and in rural areas.

Since the dismantling of apartheid, South Africa's political landscape has changed. The country was previously divided into four provinces— Cape Province, Natal, the Orange Free State, and Transvaal—and ten black homelands. Black South Africans were required to live in 10 black homelands, barren border regions located far from prosperous cities. A new constitution replaced those divisions with nine provinces: Gauteng, Northern Transvaal, Eastern Transvaal, North West, Orange Free State, KwaZulu-Natal, Eastern Cape, Northern Cape, and Western Cape.

THE PEOPLE OF SOUTH AFRICA

The ethnic diversity of South Africans is one of the country's outstanding features and a major source of conflict. The people of South Africa come from four main racial groups. Blacks make up 76 percent, and whites account for 14 percent. Coloured, people of mixed race primarily descended from the earliest immigrants and blacks, make up 9 percent, and Asians (mostly Indians) comprise 3 percent. Within these broad categories, however, there is even greater diversity and sometimes tension.

Blacks, for example, trace their origins back to many different **ethnic groups,** including Zulu, Xhosa, Pedi, Sotho, Tswana, Tsonga, Swazi, Ndebele, and Venda. The Zulus are easily the largest of the black ethnic groups and form about 22 percent of the total black population.

The Xhosa, one of the other larger groups, make up about 17.5 percent of the black population. The Xhosa were among the earliest ethnic groups to settle in South Africa, especially near Cape Town, which is located in the southwestern part of the country. Nelson Mandela, South Africa's first black president, traces his roots back to early Xhosa rulers.

Within the black population, rivalry exists between the ANC, led by Nelson Mandela, a Xhosa, and the Inkatha Freedom Party (IFP), a political party led by Zulu chief Mangosuthu Buthelezi. The conflict between these two groups has a long history that began with a disagreement over the best way to counter apartheid.

The ANC fought to create a nonracial South Africa where people of all races would be treated equally. The IFP was more concerned with protecting the freedom and independence of the Zulu kingdom in the province of Natal. Fighting between the supporters of the ANC and the IFP still rages in KwaZulu-Natal, a province stretching along South Africa's eastern seaboard. Estimates suggest that more than 14,000 people have been killed in clashes between supporters of the ANC and the IFP.

The nation's white population is also ethnically diverse, with two major groups. Afrikaners and English-speaking South Africans

IFP members fled as ANC supporters fired shots during a march in Johannesburg in early 1994. During this clash, at least 16 people were killed and 50 were injured.

have been rivals since the arrival of the British in South Africa in the late 1700s. Afrikaners make up about 60 percent of the total white population and were among the earliest white pioneers and farmers to settle in South Africa. They are primarily of Dutch descent, but often have German, French, or Flemish ancestry as well. Most Afrikaners are from the working class, have conservative political views, and identify strongly with their ethnic and cultural heritage. Afrikaners speak Afrikaans—a mixture of Dutch, German, French, Flemish, and African languages—and see themselves as a distinct group of whites within South Africa.

English-speaking whites comprise the second-largest group of white South Africans. They are more likely to be politically and socially liberal. They tend to identify themselves as South Africans—not as English-speaking South Africans or white South Africans.

Of these two groups, the Afrikaners are the larger and were once the more cohesive group politically, while the English control more of the country's financial resources.

Afrikaner farmers harvest grapes in the Cape region. The curved gables above the front door of the farmhouse are an architectural detail that early Dutch settlers brought to South Africa.

South African Tourism Board

For the most part, English-speaking South Africans and Afrikaners maintain a distant, yet civil, relationship.

Under the apartheid government, people were classified as Coloured if they were of mixed race: part white and part black, part black and part Asian, or part Asian and part white. During apartheid, many Coloured people were able to blend into white society. While they also faced discrimination, Coloureds had better access to jobs and education than blacks did.

Most of South Africa's Asian population are descendants of Indian laborers who were originally brought to the country in the 1860s to work on English sugarcane plantations. Yet two other groups are also significant: Malays, whose ancestors were imported as slaves, and Chinese descendants of those who worked in gold and diamond mines.

Many Asians prospered within their tight-knit communities by starting their own businesses. Some Afrikaner groups resented Asian prosperity, however. During the apartheid era, the government bulldozed entire Asian neighborhoods and forced the inhabitants to relocate to other areas of the country.

TENSION REMAINS

Since the collapse of the apartheid system, tension lingers between many whites and nonwhites. Although black South Africans have political control of the country, whites still own and run most businesses and have a much higher standard of living than nonwhites. The income gap between whites and nonwhites in South Africa remains significant. Whites still have greater access to education, social services, and housing. As blacks, Coloureds, and Asians gain greater educational and economic opportunities, some Afrikaners have expressed resentment and concern about their own economic future in a black-led country.

In the new South Africa, tensions also persist between the nation's Coloured population and both whites and blacks. Some Coloured groups are concerned that their interests are not always fully considered by the government because they are not "black enough." Riots and demonstrations over this issue have broken out in Johannesburg and other cities.

Because some Coloured South Africans distrust both white and black leaders, they have formed their own, ethnically based political party called the Coloured Resistance Movement. There is conflict within this group between those who want the party to focus on promoting Coloured interests and culture and those fighting for a separate Coloured homeland.

Reuters/Corbis-Bettmann

A South African of Asian descent helps a customer in a Johannesburg fruit shop.

WHO LIVES WHERE

Under apartheid the government decided where people could live based on their ethnic background. Officials removed nonwhites from South Africa's prosperous urban areas and forced them to relocate to poor, remote townships and homelands (once called Bantustans).

Because apartheid has been abolished, blacks, whites, Asians, and Coloureds are all free to reside anywhere in South Africa. Many blacks flocked into cities and now live in a new generation of shantytowns. The rest of the country's black population, however, still live in the poorer, rural parts of the country, while whites remain in affluent suburbs. The Zulu primarily inhabit the eastern province of KwaZulu-Natal, which borders the Indian Ocean. This region has been the traditional Zulu home for hundreds of years. About 80 percent of South Africa's Coloured population lives in the Western Cape province. A majority of the Asian population reside in the southern part of KwaZulu-Natal. Many Afrikaners make their homes in the provinces of Northern Transvaal, Eastern Transvaal, and North West, while most white South Africans of British descent dwell in the country's major metropolitan areas.

ECONOMY

South Africa is a modern industrial nation with a diverse economic base. Mining, manufacturing, and agriculture are the three pillars of South Africa's economic strength. In 1993 the nation's gross domestic product (GDP)—the combined value of all goods and services produced within the country in a year—was $111.8 billion. This makes South Africa one of the biggest economic powers in Africa. Large corporations owned by white elites still control most of South Africa's wealth, while the vast majority of blacks live in poverty.

South Africa's economic prosperity began in the mid to late 1800s, when miners discovered an abundance of gold and other precious minerals. South Africa is still the world's leading producer of gold and diamonds and ranks high in its output of chrome, platinum, and manganese. These minerals have impor-tant industrial uses in the United States and other highly developed nations.

Before World War II (1939–1945), precious mineral riches were South Africa's main source of economic wealth. In the past 50 years, however, manufacturing has played a larger role in the economy and accounts for about 25 percent of the country's total economic output. Important manufactured goods include machinery and transportation equipment, chemical products, synthetic fuels and petroleum products, iron and steel, processed food and beverages, paper, and textiles. Cape Town, Johannesburg, Durban, and Port Elizabeth are the country's major manufacturing centers.

Agriculture makes up about 6 percent of the nation's gross domestic product. South Africa is the leading producer of agricultural products and fertilizer in southern Africa. Major crops include sugarcane, corn, wheat, citrus fruits, cotton, tobacco, and grapes. Because of unpredictable rainfall patterns, only about 15 percent of the land is suitable for farming, and crops must rely heavily on irrigation. About 90 percent of agricultural land is devoted to raising livestock. White elites operate most of the country's large, modern farms while blacks are farmhands or operate smaller farms and rely on traditional methods that can be less productive.

The South African economy suffered a major blow between 1986 and 1990, when 25 countries enforced economic sanctions to bring down the apartheid regime. When sanctions brought the South African economy to a standstill, the apartheid government began to repeal laws designed to segregate ethnic groups. South Africa still seeks investors to strengthen its economic base.

LOOKING AHEAD
Political reformers in South Africa have made great progress. Apartheid has been abolished, and a new, permanent constitution, passed in May 1996, declares that all South Africans—regardless of race, creed, color, religion, gender, or sexual orientation—are equal under the law.

Yet democracy has created some serious challenges for South Africa's diverse society. It requires leaders of many ethnic and interest groups to set aside their differences and together tackle the political, social, and economic problems that South Africa faces. For democracy to succeed, all groups must be willing to compromise to reach solutions.

Given the history of disagreement and conflict between many of these groups, reaching a consensus is not easy. Most South Africans have demonstrated the ability to cooperate in the spirit of the common good. The future holds both challenge and promise. As the world watches, the story of South Africa continues to unfold. ⊕

At a jewelry complex in Johannesburg, a worker polishes a diamond—one of South Africa's leading exports.

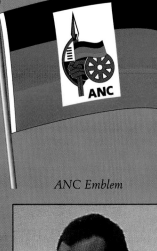

ANC Emblem

MAJOR PLAYERS IN THE CONFLICT

African National Congress   The first political party to be voted into office after the all-race elections in April 1994. The group nonviolently opposed apartheid until the Sharpeville massacre in 1960, when it turned to more violent action. When the South African government banned the ANC in 1960, they went underground. The ANC was legalized in 1990 when Nelson Mandela and other leaders were released from prison.

Buthelezi, Mangosuthu   Leader of the Inkatha Freedom Party and a cabinet member in the new government. Buthelezi has been a chief of the Buthelezi Zulu tribe since 1953.

de Klerk, F.W.   A member of the National Party and president of South Africa from 1989 through 1994. Shortly after taking office, de Klerk lifted the ban on anti-apartheid groups and released from prison Nelson Mandela and other detainees. In August 1997, de Klerk retired from politics after refusing to testify about his involvement in or knowledge of crimes committed by his government during the apartheid era.

Mangosuthu Buthelezi

F.W. de Klerk

Inkatha Freedom Party   A predominantly Zulu party dedicated to maintaining control of KwaZulu-Natal, the Zulu homeland.

Mbeki, Thabo   Deputy president of South Africa. Mbeki was chosen by Mandela to lead the ANC and to be the ANC candidate for president in 1999.

Mandela, Nelson   As the leader of the ANC, Mandela became the first black president of South Africa in 1994. During apartheid Mandela was sentenced to life imprisonment for sabotage. Mandela and his then-wife, Winnie, came to symbolize the struggle for freedom against white minority rule.

National Party   Led by F.W. de Klerk until he retired in August 1997, the National Party introduced apartheid when it came to power in 1948. The party drew most of its support from the minority Afrikaner population.

Tutu, Archbishop Desmond   An Anglican minister and outspoken member of the anti-apartheid movement. Tutu played an important role in highlighting the injustices of the apartheid system to audiences in the United States and Europe. Tutu was chosen to head the Truth and Reconciliation hearings in 1996.

IFP Emblem

Nelson Mandela

NP Emblem

THE RECENT CONFLICT AND ITS EFFECTS

May 10, 1994, is a date many South Africans and people around the world will never forget. On that day, Nelson Mandela, a leader of the anti-apartheid movement who spent nearly 30 years in jail for his cause, became the country's first black president. At his inaugural address, Mandela said, "The time for the healing of wounds has come. We pledge ourselves to liberate all our people from the continuing bondage of poverty, deprivation, suffering, gender and other discrimination."

This positive image of South Africa remains ingrained in the minds of people around the world. Aside from the occasional news of high crime rates and of political and economic breakthroughs, the public hears little these days about events in South Africa. In fact, people may be led to believe that

Two South Africans celebrate Nelson Mandela's victory. The woman on the left holds the multicolored national flag, while the other waves the flag of the ANC. In 1997 the government unveiled a new South African flag, featuring a large sun with brightly colored rays.

all of the country's apartheid-related problems have been solved. Although Mandela's election symbolized the arrival of full democracy in South Africa, the new government inherited many difficult problems.

VIOLENCE CONTINUES

Ethnic, racial, and economic conflicts continue to dominate South Africa, creating major challenges for leaders as they search for common ground on which to solve social, political, and economic dilemmas. While political violence dramatically decreased during the mid 1990s, the rivalry and fighting between the ANC and the IFP have remained a part of daily life in the remote hills of KwaZulu-Natal. On December 25, 1995, for example, several hundred Zulus supporting the IFP attacked the village of Izingolweni—an ANC strong-

Followers of the ANC and the Azanian People's Organization pull the body of a fellow supporter killed in one of many skirmishes with the IFP. The two groups were fighting over land in the mining township of Bekkersda, near Johannesburg.

hold—burning homes and hunting down villagers. The fighting left 18 dead. These violent clashes reflect ongoing conflict between the two groups over South Africa's future. The ANC wants to unify all South Africans under one government. The IFP wants self-rule in KwaZulu-Natal. Although both groups are responsible for outbreaks of violence, the IFP starts most exchanges, and the ANC responds with attacks of its own.

These outbursts of violence don't often make the front pages, even of South African newspapers, because their victims are afraid to report the attacks. Villagers who've lost their homes and family members fear revenge killings when their attackers are released from prison. Yet the number of politically motivated deaths in the province has been substantial. Between the time Mandela was elected in April 1994 and January 1996, the Human Rights Committee, an organization that monitors political violence around the world, reported that more than 1,400 people were killed in KwaZulu-Natal, an average of more than 70 per month. Reverend Dan Chetty—the director of Practical Ministries, an organization that runs educational programs in the province—summed up the situation in KwaZulu-Natal: "We have a bloody civil war here, and no one wants to admit it. Everyone wants to applaud our new democracy."

NEW PROBLEMS

Crime has become a national epidemic and is often the topic of conversation in South Africa. Since the black majority government has

> *"We have a bloody civil war here, and no one wants to admit it. Everyone wants to applaud our new democracy."*

come to power, South Africans have had unreasonable expectations of rapid change. The lack of substantial improvement in living conditions has been a source of great anger, particularly among black teenage boys living in poverty. Because they see little hope for a better life, they express their frustration with violence. **Militia groups** organized by young people disrupt life in black communities and are responsible for much of the violence in the townships.

But no one is immune to the violence. Carjackings, rapes, burglaries, and homicides affect black, white, Asian, and Coloured South Africans daily. In fact, carjackings are so common that Johannesburg's traffic chief once told drivers to approach intersections with caution and to proceed through red lights if they fear an attack. Johannesburg has one of the highest murder rates in the world. South Africa's crime problem is compounded by the police force's inability to counter it.

South Africa's understaffed, undertrained, and underpaid police force is not prepared to fight crime. For more than 40 years, police were trained to counter riots and to suppress nonwhite revolts rather than to protect the rights of all people. As a result, South Africa's police force hasn't learned how to solve crimes. During apartheid the police often forced suspects to confess by torturing and beating them rather than by conducting investigations. The Crime Information Management Center, an organization that monitors crime in South Africa, reports that between 1993 and 1996, the number of cases that had not been solved had risen by 55 percent over previous years. To make matters worse, police themselves are sometimes the criminals. Homicide and attempted homicide rates are higher among the police force than they are among the general population.

The frustration of watching many criminals go free after repeated offenses has prompted private citizens to hire personal security guards. High walls topped with razor wire fortify and protect the homes of the rich from intruders. The poor, however, who are more often the victims of random acts of violence, have little protection against crime. Some poor communities have taken matters into their own hands and have turned to **vigilante** justice. In Cape Town, a group called People Against Gangsterism and Drugs was responsible for killing a well-known gang leader in August 1996.

Poor South Africans continue to hope that President Mandela will make a difference, but their patience is wearing thin. "It's taking too long," a Johannesburg woman told a reporter for *The New York Times*. "The government said they would give us security, but there is no security."

INEQUALITIES REMAIN
Although the new government has begun the enormous task of further

dismantling the apartheid system and of addressing its lingering impact on South African society, apartheid-era divisions run deep. Race and ethnicity still divide South Africans and shape the nation's most important political, economic, and social debates. During the apartheid years, South Africa's government did everything in its power to widen the gap between whites and nonwhites. By law whites were guaranteed the best education and training, and the highest-paying jobs. The white-minority government spent 12 times more money to educate white students than it did to educate black students. Black teachers taught in crowded classrooms, with up to four times as many students as there were in white classrooms.

Because of these poor conditions, less than 50 percent of black South Africans have

South African police tried to restrain a trade union member who was participating in a peaceful march through Pretoria in March 1990.

Archive Photos/Paul Velasco/Reuters

In May 1997, the South African government appointed Meyer Kahn, chairman of South African Breweries, to serve as the new chief of the national police force. Government officials hoped that the appointment of Kahn, a tough, no-nonsense businessman, would be seen as a bold move to finally do something about the mounting crime problem. Kahn certainly had his work cut out for him. At the time of his appointment, the World Economic Forum had just ranked South Africa along with Russia and Colombia as countries most severely in the grip of organized crime. McKinsey and Company, a U.S.-based consulting firm, found South Africa's police force to be a case study in bad management.

An editorial in the *Star,* a prominent South African newspaper, summed up the country's hopes for its new police chief: "Meyer Kahn is no ordinary businessman. Organiser extraordinaire, [he] is blessed with vision and [is] unimpeded by boardroom pretensions. He aims to reorganise the service, improve morale and put the [police] force on a proper footing to reclaim our society from the thugs. . . . Kahn has a fighting chance given the support not only of the Government and the police hierarchy, but of the public too."

learned to read and write, while all but 1 percent of whites are literate. Inferior education translates into fewer opportunities for good jobs. Adult blacks earn less than one-third of the salaries of their white peers, and blacks are eight times more likely to be unemployed. Health care available to non-whites is also inferior to the care that whites receive. The infant mortality rate for blacks is more than 50 percent and is almost 40 percent for Coloureds, compared to more than 8 percent for whites and about 10 percent for Asians.

Although laws that once segregated black and white residential areas have been repealed, few neighborhoods are integrated. Whites generally live in large cities, close to where they work, while blacks remain in outlying townships. Some blacks who are better off financially have fled the townships for more affluent white suburbs. One-fourth of all blacks live in rundown housing in crime-ridden neighborhoods or have no housing at all. And it could get worse. Experts predict that by the year 2000, 3 million black South Africans

During apartheid black students crowded into dark classrooms that had few books or other learning tools. Whites, on the other hand, were able to study in the finest libraries and to be taught by well-trained teachers.

will need housing, compared to 500,000 people in all other ethnic groups combined. Forty percent of blacks lack access to clean water, and only 33 percent of black homes have electricity. In contrast, very few whites live in homes without electricity or running water.

REFORM

All this creates a daunting picture, and the government's response has only begun to scratch the surface. The Reconstruction and Development Program (RDP) is the cornerstone for reform in South Africa. The RDP announced ambitious plans to build new homes, schools, hospitals, and paved roads; to bring electricity and running water to rural areas; to reduce crime; to reorganize the educational system; and to redistribute land.

In addition to promoting economic development and equality, the government has established the Truth and Reconciliation Commission (TRC), lead by Archbishop Desmond Tutu, to address the emotional wounds of South Africans. The TRC was charged with investigating human-rights abuses that had occurred under apartheid. Because the goal of the hearings was to get all confessions out in the open, it was announced that of those who came forward to confess, most would not be prosecuted for their crimes. In January 1997, five former police officers admitted during hearings that in 1977 they had beaten and killed Steven Biko, the charismatic young leader of the Black Consciousness Movement (BCM). (Biko's death while in police custody had raised an international outcry

Kids play at a construction site in Soweto township. Although the government announced plans to build 1 million houses in 5 years, only 123,000 had been constructed by 1997.

1996, the government proposed a land-reform program to give back land that apartheid laws had taken away from black South Africans. By March 1997, however, *The New York Times* reported that only 1 percent of the land had actually been transferred.

RESISTANCE TO CHANGE

In a country with an ethnic population as diverse as South Africa's, it's not surprising that not all South Africans welcome reform. Afrikaner groups, for example, have mounted strong resistance to the government's effort to integrate public and private schools. In some cases, Afrikaner parents have withdrawn their children to protest the inclusion of black, Coloured, and Asian students in formerly all-white schools. In other cases, Afrikaner parents have put up barricades to keep out black students. South Africa's Supreme Court had to force angry Afrikaner parents to integrate a school in the town of Potgietersrus, located in Northern Transvaal Province.

The government's attempts to provide more opportunities for black South

WENKOMMANDO

Archive Photos/Express Newspapers

A young member of the neo-nazi Afrikaner Resistance Movement (AWB) showed his opposition to the 1994 all-race elections by prominently displaying the organization's flag.

against apartheid policies, but the police claimed that Biko had killed himself by beating his head against a cement wall.)

Despite the government's reform plans many South Africans feel that progress has been too slow. The RDP has not been able to build as many new houses, schools, or hospitals as hoped. The government promised to provide 1 million houses in five years, but as of 1997, only 123,000 had been constructed. Nor has the government dramatically improved living conditions for poor South Africans, who received only about 3 percent of the government's first budget. In February

Africans has threatened some Afrikaners. While South Africa's constitution guarantees equal rights for all, it also provides "for the protection and advancement of the disadvantaged majority." This policy upsets many white and Coloured groups, who see the policy as a way to give less-qualified blacks preferential treatment for jobs in government and private industry. Some jobs require applicants to speak an African language, a skill that virtually no whites, Coloureds, or Asians possess. In response, groups such as the all-white Mine Worker's Union have gone to court to stop policies that set aside some government jobs specifically for blacks. These groups claim that South Africa's nonblacks are at a disadvantage when competing for jobs.

In February 1997, riots broke out in Eldorado Park, a mixed-race township located 30 miles south of Johannesburg. Protesters claimed that the government was discriminating against Coloured and other nonblack South Africans. The demonstrators quoted higher rates of unemploy-

ment and inferior education and health care as evidence of their claim. As one protester told a reporter for the Associated Press, mixed-race South Africans are "not black enough and not white enough" to have a place in the new South Africa. Rioters looted shops and homes, burned tires, and fought with police.

COALITION DISSOLVES

In the mid 1990s, pictures of Mandela clasping hands with F.W. de Klerk, the last apartheid-era president, were powerful symbols in a nation torn by years of bitter racial and ethnic fighting. De Klerk's National Party won enough parliamentary seats in the 1994 elections to form a coalition government with Mandela. This cooperation between former enemies raised the possibility that all South Africans could build a new nation.

By May 1996, however, the coalition had dissolved. De Klerk resigned as deputy president and announced that he and six other National Party ministers were pulling out of the government. According to de Klerk, the Nationalists felt that they no longer were able

to play a meaningful role in a government dominated by the ANC, although others believe the NP was positioning itself for the next election.

While Mandela called the decision to leave "regrettable," he and other (ANC) government leaders had expected it for some time. "We are not taking this decision in a negative spirit. . . . We are not sour," Mandela said in a news conference. "We believe that the development of a strong and vigilant opposition is essential for the maintenance and promotion of genuine multiparty democracy. We have reached a natural watershed in the transformation of our society."

Meanwhile, relations between the ANC and the IFP remain tense. The 1994 elections also gave the IFP enough parliamentary clout to join the coalition. IFP leader Buthelezi resists any loss of power to a national government and often threatens to walk out of Parliament. The future of IFP participation in the national government remains in doubt and historic differences among South Africa's people continue to cast a long shadow.

CHAPTER 1   *The Recent Conflict and Its Effects*

CHAPTER

2

THE CONFLICT'S ROOTS

To better understand the racial and ethnic conflicts in South Africa, it's important to look at the past. For South African students, this hasn't always been possible. During apartheid, teachers across the country offered students a distorted version of their history, a version that skipped over the thousands of years before white people arrived on the continent.

EARLY HISTORY

About 8000 B.C., the Khoisan, a nomadic group of hunter-gatherers, traveled throughout the southern part of the African continent, searching for water and wild game. Each band claimed an extensive area as its hunting grounds. If one group wanted to cross into another's territory, the group's members had to formally request permission. Crossing a boundary without proper consent often caused fighting between the bands.

The Khoisan, who were famous for the cave paintings they left in the mountains of southern Africa, valued their freedom and their independent way of life. The people had a strong sense of community and co-

An illustration shows Khoisan hunters scouting a valley for game.

operation. Khoisan men hunted, while women gathered fruits, berries, melons, and nuts.

When drought conditions hindered gathering, some Khoisan turned to raising and herding cattle, sheep, and goats for food. Because they had more control over their food supply than the hunting and gathering Khoisan, these herders lived in more permanent settlements. The people moved when they needed to find fresh pastureland for their animals.

A second major ethnic group, unrelated to the Khoisan, first arrived in South Africa between A.D. 100 and A.D. 300. They had come from farther north, in search of water, pastures, and farmland. These people, thought to be ancestors of present-day Bantu-speaking groups,

Archive Photos

© Jason Laure

Above: *The Khoisan traveled with cattle through areas of what would become Lesotho, South Africa, and Swaziland. Left: The Khoisan left behind clues to their lives in caves and on rocks throughout South Africa. They mixed iron oxide, egg white, and plant sap to create the images of the brownish red animals that they saw on their hunt.*

Zulu chiefs encouraged warriors before an attack. Although most Zulu carried traditional spears, some had guns, which were introduced to native South Africans by Europeans.

Stock Montage

grew much of their own food, made tools from iron, and built sturdy, permanent houses. From A.D. 100 to about A.D. 1500, the Bantu-speaking population grew rapidly and pushed farther into southern Africa.

Several Bantu-speaking groups settled in areas of present-day KwaZulu-Natal and Eastern Cape Province. The southward migration of the Bantu-speaking peoples created a mini population explosion that forced the newcomers to compete with the Khoisan for land. The Bantu-speakers drove many of the Khoisan farther south and west, while integrating others into their group. The largest of the Bantu-speaking groups was the Nguni, which included the Xhosa. The Xhosa, one of the most powerful subgroups, eventually occu-

pied large areas in the Eastern Cape, where they herded cattle and grew crops.

By A.D. 1500, the Khoisan and the Bantu-speaking peoples were firmly established in different areas of South Africa. At the time, the total population in this area may have numbered between 100,000 and 200,000. These peoples had little or no contact with the outside world.

EUROPEANS ARRIVE

Geography played an important role in drawing Euro-

pean explorers to South Africa. In the late 1400s, Portuguese sailors frequently sailed around the Cape of Good Hope, at the southern tip of South Africa, on their trading journeys between Portugal and Asia. The Portuguese traded iron and copper goods for silks and spices, which were highly valued throughout Europe.

Although the voyages were profitable, they were also long and difficult. During their many months at sea, sailors often grew sick and died from a disease called scurvy. Sailors began stopping midway through the long trip at the Cape of Good Hope to rest, restock the food supply, and tend to the sick. By the late 1500s, English and Dutch sailors also began to use the Cape of Good Hope as a rest stop on their way to and from Asia.

In 1652 agents of the wealthy and powerful Dutch East India Company, which imported silks and spices from Asia, decided to establish a permanent refreshment station at the Cape. The company sent Jan van Riebeeck to set up a fort and a hospital and to start supplying fresh meat, fruit, and vegetables to sailors. The small settlement grew quickly as van Riebeeck and the colonists built a fort, planted orchards, and seized land from the Khoisan to create farms for cattle.

At first the Khoisan accepted the presence of a few white immigrants in their homeland. At the same time, the European settlers developed a trading relationship with the Xhosa. The traders traveled east of the Great Fish River to exchange glass beads and iron nails for ivory and

Laden with supplies and food, a British ship leaves the Cape Town settlement.

Courtesy of Peabody Essex Museum of Salem

Trade between the Khoisan and Europeans in the Western Cape wasn't always peaceful. European traders often chased away or killed the Khoisan before taking what they wanted.

cattle. But the Khoisan and the Xhosa soon realized that the growing white presence endangered their livelihoods. For example, Europeans continued to take over Khoisan and Xhosa land.

The first clashes between whites and African peoples in South Africa occurred because of disputes over cattle and land. The Khoisan cattle herders launched raids and rebellions to stop the Dutch from taking Khoisan land. The Khoisan wanted the Dutch to leave the Cape. At the same time, the hunting and gathering Khoisan, who had no notion of owning animals or property, further angered the immigrants by hunting their cattle for food.

When the Dutch responded by attacking the Khoisan in 1659, they began an era of low-intensity warfare. While the Khoisan fought back, they were quickly overwhelmed by the superior weapons of the whites. Following their victory, the Dutch seized even more grazing lands beyond the Cape Peninsula. Most of the surviving Khoisan eventually migrated to other parts of southern Africa, while others fled north to the Kalahari Desert. Africans who remained in the Cape settlement in time became the paid servants of the Dutch.

Meanwhile, the Dutch East India Company did not have enough farmers to keep up with the sailors' demand for crops. When the Dutch tried to enslave the Khoisan, they resisted, prompting the Dutch to import slaves into the region from other parts of Africa, including Mozambique and Madagascar, and from Indonesia and India in Asia. As the Cape settlement grew, the Dutch brought in more slaves to farm the land. Soon the economy of the Cape settlement became dependent upon slave labor. Without African and Asian slaves, white landowners in the Cape would not have been able to operate their large farms (and white attitudes that they were superior to nonwhites may not have been as pronounced later on.)

To bring ever-higher crop yields, the Dutch promised free land to other Europeans who immigrated to the Cape settlement and agreed to farm. The Dutch were soon joined by Flemish, Scandinavian, French, and German immigrants. Most of these immigrants were poor and came hoping to find a better life in a new land. Many of the French were Huguenots—Protestants who were fleeing religious persecution in France. In time, Dutch, French, and German colonists, mainly farmers and cattle herders, became known as **Boers,** the Dutch word for farmers. The Boers eventually developed their own distinctive culture, including their own language, Afrikaans—which distinguished the Boers from other European-descended groups.

As white settlement continued, Cape Town became a major European stop along the trade route to Asia. Although the Dutch East India Company had never intended to establish a colony at the Cape, the settlement grew as more immigrants arrived and took over more land. As the settlers moved eastward from the Cape settlement, they continued to clash with the Khoisan over land.

By the end of the seventeenth century, the Khoisan had lost most of their lands and had sold many of their cattle. Sicknesses such as smallpox, unknowingly carried by the Europeans, killed many Khoisan because they had no natural resistance. More Khoisan died from a lack of food. The few remaining Khoisan women often settled down and had children with Dutch men. The children of these mixed relationships became known as Coloureds.

EXPANSION CONTINUES

Although poor, many of the early European immigrants to South Africa were independent and adventurous farmers who wanted to live outside the influence of the powerful Dutch East India Company. In the 1770s, those who wanted nothing to do with the Dutch settlements loaded up their ox-driven covered wagons and headed north and east, away from Cape Town.

The Dutch called these adventurers trekboers, an Afrikaans word that means "traveling farmers." Trekboers were very religious and strongly identified with the biblical stories of Israel. These people drew inspiration from the ancient Israelites and sought a promised land where they could live according to their own religious standards. Some also considered the dark-skinned people they encountered on their trek to be the forces of evil because they prevented the Boers from happily settling in their new land. (This prejudice would carry over to later generations of trekboers.)

As they moved farther from the Cape settlement, the trekboers encountered

This Khoisan woman chose to stay in the Cape settlement and adjust to the European way of life. She wears European-style clothes.

resistance from the Khoisan, and the Xhosa who fought hard to defend their land. The trekboers clashed with these ethnic groups, launching a series of raids, skirmishes, and all-out battles over territory. The trekboers defeated the small numbers of Khoisan fighters relatively quickly. The Xhosa, on the other hand, waged war against the trekboers for several decades in a series of wars. Most fighting resulted from Boer efforts to push Xhosa groups from lands west of the Great Fish River. After the fifth war, Xhosa and Boer leaders established a neutral zone between the Great Fish and the Keiskamm Rivers, where no Xhosa or Boers could settle.

BRITISH RULE

Great Britain took active steps to secure its interest in Southern Africa. They wanted the region for two reasons. First, the area could provide a secure and strategic naval base for its large fleet. Second, the Cape settlement could be- come an important market for the manufactured goods being pumped out of British factories.

Wars in Europe served Britain's plans in Africa. In the mid 1790s, France invaded the Netherlands, and British troops seized control of many Dutch colonies, including the Cape settlement.

British law governed the European and non-European populations and affected them in many ways. The British abolished the slave trade in 1807, so no addi-

A Boer family heads away from Cape Town in an ox-driven wagon to escape British rule.

North Wind Picture Archives

tional slaves could be brought into the settlement. Existing slaves, however, remained unpaid laborers on Boer estates. In 1809 new laws required blacks and Coloureds to carry passes that verified their residence and terms of employment. People needed state permission to move or to change jobs. Although partly intended to prevent employers from exploiting workers, the law indirectly forced blacks to take the only jobs available—working for white farmers.

Beginning in 1813, the British enforced laws requiring slaveholders to treat their slaves fairly. This meant slaves could take their masters to court whenever they had claims of abuse. Boers were particularly upset by this law and didn't believe that slaves should have any voice in court at all.

Meanwhile, to settle conflicts between Boers and Xhosa on the eastern frontier, the British devised the settlement scheme of 1820. It established several British settlements close together on small plots of farmland in the neutral zone. The British hoped the scheme would se-

cure the area against Xhosa attacks and divide the Boer settlements. Under the plan, thousands of British colonists flooded into South Africa. English became the Cape Colony's official language in 1822, and the Khoisan were given protection from human-rights abuses. In 1828 Ordinance 50 granted Coloureds the right to own land, abolished the need for them to carry passes, and granted them freedom of movement within the colony. This law greatly upset the Boers who relied on the cheap supply of Coloured labor to run their farms. In 1833 Great Britain outlawed slavery in all British colonies, including the Cape. By 1838, all slaves were allowed to go free.

At the same time, drought and overpopulation caused conflict between Nguni bands. The rise of the pow-

erful Zulu ruler Shaka in present-day KwaZulu-Natal pushed other Nguni and Bantu-speaking groups from the area. Most went north into what would become Mozambique, Zimbabwe, and Botswana. European slave raids in the area added to the conflict. The forced removal of other African groups by Zulus and fighting between groups continued until 1837 and came to be known as *mfecane*, the Nguni term for "the crushing." The warring between Nguni tribes produced a number of powerful chiefdoms including the Swazi, Lesotho, and Ndebele. All of these groups were able to give serious resistance to white expansion in the nineteenth century.

THE GREAT TREK
Boer farmers who relied on slave labor to work their farms bitterly resented what

Cecil John Rhodes was in the right place at the right time when diamonds were first discovered in the Cape Colony in the late 1860s and early 1870s. Born in England, Rhodes was 17 years old when he was sent to live with his brother in South Africa in 1870. Intrigued by the nearby diamond discoveries, Rhodes became a diamond prospector and quickly struck it rich. He developed a lifelong interest in southern Africa.

After making his fortune, Rhodes returned to England and enrolled at Oxford University. At the same time, he maintained his interests in the diamond business and frequently traveled back and forth between England and southern Africa. Between 1873 and 1881, Rhodes aggressively consolidated a large number of mining claims in the region to form the powerful De Beers Mining Company, which he controlled. In 1881, he was elected to a seat in the Cape Colony Parliament, a post which he held for the remainder of his life.

Rhodes was a strong believer in the superiority of British culture and was convinced that Great Britain should play a dominant role in the development of southern Africa. Throughout his life, he was a tireless promoter of efforts to increase Great Britain's control over the region. He was largely responsible for the British annexation of Bechuanaland (now Botswana) in 1885. Through the British South Africa Company, which Rhodes founded, he exercised control over the regions of present-day Zimbabwe and Zambia—an area which the British government later (1894) named Rhodesia, in Rhodes's honor.

In 1890, Rhodes was elected premier of the Cape Colony. His efforts to expand British influence in the region soon brought him into direct conflict with the Boers in the Transvaal. Rhodes had long encouraged British colonization of South Africa, even advocating the construction of a railroad line extending from Cape Town to Cairo, Egypt. This aggressive stance infuriated the Boers, who were already wary of British ambitions in the region. As British miners flooded into the Transvaal, tension between the Boers and the British "Uitlanders" (Afrikaans for foreigners) mounted.

In 1895, Rhodes backed an unsuccessful invasion of Transvaal. While he had been a chief sponsor of the action, he was acquitted of responsibility. Nevertheless, he was officially rebuked in Parliament and forced to resign as Cape Colony Premier. Rhodes devoted the rest of his life to the development of Rhodesia. He died in 1902 and left most of his large fortune to Oxford University, which used his gift to establish the Rhodes scholarships.

Independent Picture Service

they regarded as British interference in their affairs. The Boers felt that the British were destroying the fabric of their society and threatening their economic survival. In response, from 1838 to 1839, six to eight thousand Boers moved north and east of the Cape Colony in what became known as the Great Trek (Voortrek). Voortrekkers attacked the lands inhabited by the Lesotho, Ndebele, Zulu, and Pedi as they went, taking control of some of the groups' lands. Boer-Zulu fighting was especially intense in present-day Transvaal and KwaZulu-Natal. After some early victories, the Zulus were decisively beaten by the Boers at a battle on the Ncome River in 1838.

Meanwhile, the British continued to dominate most parts of southern Africa. British forces occupied the coastal region of Natal,

Left: *A political cartoon depicts Cecil Rhodes straddling the African continent from Cape Town to Cairo (in Egypt), two cities he wanted to connect by rail.*

where they established a British colony in 1843. The British advanced along the eastern Cape frontier and eventually intruded on Xhosa lands, sparking several wars. In 1848 British troops gained control of the Orange River territory, where Boers had settled.

As the British and the Boers continued to compete for land and resources, the British accepted the independence of the two Boer republics—the Transvaal, located north of the Vaal River, and the Orange Free State, located between the Orange and Vaal Rivers. By 1854 southern Africa was divided into two Boer republics and two British colonies, the Cape and Natal. Although attempts to unite the Transvaal and the Orange Free State failed, the two Boer republics maintained ties.

RICHES AND WARFARE

The discovery of southern Africa's rich mineral resources, especially gold and diamonds, opened a new chapter in the already tense relationship between the British and the Boers. In 1867 two young Boer children, Erasmus and Louisa Jacobs, picked up a shiny pebble close to the south banks of the Orange River. After refinement, the children's toy turned out to be a 21-carat diamond. A few years later, in 1871, miners found gold deposits in the Transvaal. These and later discoveries rekindled Britain's interest in the African interior. In response, large numbers of British adventurers migrated to the Transvaal in 1877 to seek their fortunes. Britain soon passed laws to annex the Transvaal and gain control over the new-found riches, a move that upset many Boers. The mineral discoveries sparked the industrialization of South Africa.

During the same period, Britain continued to conquer black ethnic groups and to seize their land. By 1880 British forces had defeated the Zulus. The Boers took advantage of Britain's distraction with the Zulu battles and declared war in 1880. After several battles in what was called the first Anglo-Boer War, the Boers defeated the British army in 1881, and Britain left Transvaal alone—for the moment. Meanwhile, the Boers came to be known as Afrikaners by

During the second Anglo-Boer War, these British lancers refused to surrender even though they were outnumbered 150 to 400. Both British and Boer sides hired or impressed thousands of blacks as laborers, dispatch-runners, and spies.

virtue of their language—Afrikaans—and membership in the Dutch Reformed church.

Conflict between the British and the Boers didn't end with the first Anglo-Boer War. When miners discovered more precious minerals in 1886, including large gold deposits near present-day Johannesburg, the British flooded into the region once again. President Paul Kruger—leader of the South African Republic, as the Transvaal was sometimes called—responded by heavily taxing British companies and by refusing to grant the British miners equal status under the law. To strengthen the Boers' position against the British, Kruger also formed an alliance with Germany, Britain's political rival.

Britain strongly objected to Kruger's treatment of British subjects and to the alliance with Germany. Between 1895 and 1896, British troops from Natal and the Cape Colony attempted to overthrow Kruger's government but failed. On October 11, 1899, the Transvaal and Orange Free State declared war on Britain, dividing southern Africa into pro-British and pro-Boer camps.

The second Anglo-Boer War (1899–1902), was a battle for

control of southern Africa. The Boers fought for their freedom and for the very existence of their republics, while the British fought to expand their empire and to protect the rights of British miners. The Boers used **guerrilla tactics** to attack the British and had some early success. The British, in turn, captured and imprisoned thousands of Boer men, women, and children, about 26,000 of whom died in British concentration camps during the war. By May 1902, British forces had prevailed and the Boers surrendered.

Under the terms of the Treaty of Vereeniging, all of South Africa—including the Transvaal and the Orange Free State—became British territory. By 1910 the British had established the Union of South Africa with four provinces—the Orange Free State, Transvaal, the Cape Colony, and Natal. English and Dutch became the country's official languages.

The Union of South Africa modeled its government after Great Britain's, with a two-chambered legislature consisting of a house and a senate. South Africa's Parliament exercised political power, and a British governor general symbolized South Africa's link to the British Empire.

PRELUDE TO APARTHEID

Discrimination against nonwhites was present long before the founding of the Union of South Africa, but the new government legalized the unfair treatment. Under the Union's new constitution, only whites could vote in three of the four provinces. In the Cape Colony, Coloureds and blacks could vote if they had the necessary property qualifications—something most nonwhites lacked. Only white representatives could serve in Parliament.

Lacking any real political power, nonwhites were easily exploited by the all-white government. Legislators passed the first of many laws intended to maintain white power and privilege and to keep blacks permanently in inferior positions. In 1911 the Mine and Works Act prevented blacks from earning certificates to perform blasting operations, reserving this

Discrimination in the Mines

To be profitable, the mining companies needed a steady supply of cheap labor. Whites were not willing to do this dangerous work unless they were well paid, so the companies turned to the government. The government imposed taxes on land owned by blacks and in many cases, seized black land altogether. Unable to farm themselves, blacks were forced to work for white farmers or to take the only other jobs available. Most of these jobs were in the mines.

There was a major difference between the working conditions of whites and of blacks. Most whites were supervisors who were fairly paid and had many opportunities for advancement. Black miners had to do the most dangerous jobs and had no opportunities to improve their prospects. Miners lived hard lives. The government set up all-male compounds, far from home and limited visits from family members. The mining companies provided free liquor to distract the miners from their difficult lives.

and other high-paying, skilled jobs for whites.

In response, black leaders organized the South African Native National Congress (SANNC) to fight for the political rights of black Africans. Members believed in peacefully working to promote black civil rights through nonviolent forms of protest, such as signing petitions and staging boycotts, sit-ins, and demonstrations.

In the same year, J.B.M. Hertzog formed the National Party, which won the support of voting Afrikaners by promising to preserve Afrikaner culture and to maintain Afrikaner economic prosperity. Hertzog feared that the less populous but more powerful British would wash away Afrikaner identity.

Meanwhile, the government passed more laws to limit the freedoms of nonwhites. The 1913 Natives' Land Act set aside less than 10 percent of South Africa's land for blacks and forbade them from moving or buying land outside set boundaries. The Immigration Act limited the movement of Asians, who responded by rioting.

The 1923 Natives (Urban Areas) Act established townships outside major cities where blacks could rent homes but could not buy them. The act enabled local governments to restrict the presence of blacks in urban areas and to deport the unemployed to the reserves. Blacks protested the new restrictions by burning their passes in public.

With these laws in place, all black communities were at the mercy of the white-ruled government. Under a section of the 1927 Black Administration Act, South Africa's president could order any community to pick up and move from one part of the country to another. Whole neighborhoods were often given less than an hour to pack what they could and board buses to the reserves or townships. Forced removals became an everyday occurrence in South Africa.

The 1929 election brought issues of race to the forefront. The National Party announced plans to achieve white dominance and criticized Jan Smuts and his more tolerant Afrikaner-led South African Party for not trying hard enough to remove from the voting rolls those blacks and Coloureds who still had voting rights in the Cape Province. In the process of winning the election, the National Party drew upon Afrikaners' antagonism towards blacks and English-speaking South Africans, establishing the party's agenda for the next several decades.

Meanwhile, the worldwide economic depression rocked South Africa. By 1934 Hertzog formed a coalition with Smuts to create the United Party, which won that year's elections at the expense of a few members. Afrikaner extremist D.F. Malan rejected the alliance and broke away to form the Purified National Party, which would form the government's main opposition for the next 14 years.

The 1913 Natives' Land Act set aside less than 10 percent of South Africa's land for blacks and forbade them from moving or buying land outside reserved boundaries.

ANC members posed for this photo in 1930. In its early years, the ANC refused to use violence to counter apartheid. The group's activity increased in the 1940s when Albert Luthuli recruited Nelson Mandela, Walter Sisulu, and Oliver Tambo.

World War II broke out in 1939, pitting Britain and its allies against Germany. Members of the Purified National Party and a semisecret **white supremacist group** called the Afrikaner Broederbond (Brotherhood) openly supported the views of German leader Adolf Hitler. Broederbond members believed that they belonged to a master race and that they were justified in treating nonwhites as inferior beings.

These extremists hoped South Africa would remain neutral and that Britain would lose to Germany, giving Nationalists a chance to turn South Africa into an Afrikaner country.

Despite Hertzog's attempts to keep South Africa neutral, Parliament narrowly voted to join the war on Britain's side, and South Africa sent 350,000 citizens to fight in Ethiopia, North Africa, and Europe.

South Africa's mineral wealth attracted several foreign investors both during and after the war. Western European and American corporations accounted for nearly 40 percent of South Africa's gross domestic investment in the years immediately following the war. The war forced South Africa to expand and to rebuild its industrial facilities to meet the demands of its own and Allied troops. As a result,

Gandhi's *Satyagraha*

Black Africans were not the only non-white group to be exploited by the all-white government of the Union of South Africa. Wealthy owners of South Africa's sugar plantations and coal mines needed cheap labor to cultivate their land and to mine their coal. As a result, they imported thousands of laborers from India, offering 10-year contracts to those who came. These Indian immigrants primarily settled in Natal, where the largest plantations and mines were located. Other Indians immigrated to South Africa to trade with the Indian labor force. Many of the Indian merchants started their own businesses and thrived.

Some English-speaking whites and Afrikaners felt threatened when the Indian population prospered and expanded. They wanted the Indians to be deported. Because India was a British colony, Indians were British subjects and therefore were free to move anywhere

Archive Photos

within the British Empire. Although the South African Parliament couldn't deport them, it treated Indians as second-class citizens and restricted them to Natal through a combination of pass laws, high taxes, and limited immigrant quotas.

In 1893 this situation came to the attention of Mohandas Gandhi, a young Indian lawyer who had come several years earlier to Durban, a large city in Natal. Gandhi's life was forever changed that year during a routine train trip from Durban to Pretoria. When the train reached Pietermaritzburg, a conductor insisted that Gandhi transfer from a "whites only" section to a third-class compartment. Gandhi refused and was kicked off the train. Gandhi later called this experience of being treated as a member of an inferior race "the most important factor" in spurring his lifelong battle for civil rights for all people.

In 1894 Gandhi founded the Natal Indian Congress (NIC), which later inspired those who founded the ANC. In the years that followed, he was often arrested for disobeying laws. Gandhi popularized *satyagraha,* or passive resistance. In practice, this meant breaking laws he viewed as unjust and accepting the consequences without fighting back. Gandhi's philosophy of nonviolent resistance to oppression inspired people struggling for civil rights throughout the world.

South Africa became dependent upon foreign money.

Fueled by foreign investments, the industrial boom brought more blacks to the cities, where they found good jobs in factories. But housing and social services for blacks did not increase to meet the demand. Cities became overcrowded, and crime rates went up. When whites returned from World War II, they went back to work in their former privileged positions. Angry blacks who had lost their wartime jobs struck in 1946. Of the 50,000 striking blacks, several hundred were killed when the government suppressed the strike. The strike increased white fears of black militancy. The National Party exploited these fears in its campaign for the 1948 elections, which they immediately began to prepare for after the United Party was reelected in 1943. The National Party also used urban overcrowding and increased crime rates as examples of what would happen to South Africa if blacks were allowed to move ahead economically.

In 1946 the National Indian Congress led a passive resistance meeting against laws restricting Indians from buying land.

Daniel F. Malan (front row, third from left) *posed with his cabinet shortly after he was elected in 1948. With the help of Hendrik Verwoerd, commonly referred to as the architect of apartheid, Malan built the apartheid state.*

The party made a program of apartheid the foundation for its campaign platform. Under apartheid, Nationalists promised that whites would have distinct advantages over blacks in the job market. But the National Party's plan did not end with employment opportunities—the proposed apartheid system reached into every aspect of South African society. Following a theory of H.F. Verwoerd, the editor of a Nationalist newspaper, the plan called for the complete separation of ethnic groups in South Africa.

While the National Party geared up for the 1948 election, more nonwhites estab-lished political action groups to protest recent laws. Coloured South Africans banded together to create the Non-European Unity Move-ment (NEUM). Founders of the group declared their in-tention to "acquire all those rights which are presently en-joyed by the European popu-lation." More specifically the group hoped to gain the right to vote (for Coloured South Africans not living in the Cape), to gain access to equal education and employment opportunities, to assert their civil rights, and to establish land ownership rights.

Meanwhile, Alfred B. Xuma, leader of the African National Congress (ANC, formerly the SANNC) began to recruit talented and ener-getic young activists to the growing protest movement. Oliver Tambo, Walter Sisulu, and Nelson Mandela, some of Xuma's recruits from the early 1940s, helped form the African National Congress Youth League (ANCYL) and soon became the organiza-tion's leading members. By the late 1940s, these and other members of ANCYL had persuaded the ANC to adopt more aggressive meth-ods of protesting unjust laws.

At the same time, India passed the first economic sanctions against South

SOUTH AFRICA   *Nation in Transition*

Africa, to protest the South African government's treatment of Asian immigrants. The sanctions did little to change the government's policy, but they attracted the attention of the United Nations Security Council, which began to keep an eye on South Africa.

APARTHEID LEGALIZED

Although racial and ethnic conflict had already been a constant theme in South African history, race relations dramatically changed in 1948 when the Afrikaner-led National Party won a crucial national election. Campaigning on a program of white supremacy and a pledge to separate whites from nonwhites in every sphere of society, Daniel F. Malan won the election by a narrow margin to become president of South Africa. Malan and his supporters openly expressed their contempt for South Africa's nonwhite population. Many white South Africans had historically sought to separate whites from blacks and to control the country's black population, but the Nationalists attempted segregation on a much broader scale. Under the National Party's programs, racial segregation became the cornerstone of the South African state, enforced by the government-controlled police force.

The Appeal of Apartheid

In the years leading up to the 1948 election, Afrikaners had become more prosperous and formal British influence had declined. But Afrikaner prosperity depended upon the preservation of the country's economic powerhouses—mainly the mining and manufacturing industries, both of which required large, cheap labor forces to succeed. The National Party's promise to limit nonwhites to unskilled, low-paying jobs guaranteed the cheap labor supply and enabled Afrikaners and other whites to enjoy a rising standard of living.

The National Party also understood Afrikaners' strong ties to independence and cultural identity. Many Afrikaners came from poor Dutch, German, Belgian, and French backgrounds. When they came to South Africa they faced the hardships of settling in a new land and of fighting British power and influence. Afrikaners had often been attacked, dispersed, and forced to withdraw from claimed lands. To survive Afrikaners banded together, developing strong religious and cultural traditions and a sense of being a chosen, superior people.

A new threat to Afrikaner security surfaced during the first half of the twentieth century, when colonies began gaining independence and greater civil rights. Afrikaners feared that if this trend came to South Africa their culture, identity, and economic status would be lost. To increase its political power, the National Party exploited this fear by supporting policies—long taught in Afrikaner schools—that ensured Afrikaner culture remained dominant in South Africa. Afrikaner religious and cultural leaders reinforced the beliefs that white Europeans were superior to black Africans and that the two races should not mix. When the National Party promised to defend Afrikaner ethnic identity, it won over the Afrikaner population, whose votes essentially carried the party into power.

CHAPTER

3

ENTRENCHED POSITIONS

Beginning in 1949, President Malan and his government passed apartheid laws. The first law, the Prohibition of Mixed Marriages and Immorality Act, made it a crime (punishable by seven years in prison) for blacks and whites to marry or to have sexual relations. More laws soon followed. The Group Areas Act of 1950 defined where people could and could not live. The Population Registration Act divided South Africans into four racial categories— white, black, Coloured, and Asian—and required nonwhites to carry documents as proof of their category. Husbands, wives, and children were often separated when

bureaucrats classified family members into different groups based on language ability, skin color, and curliness of hair.

Under apartheid the government strengthened its enforcement of earlier laws by seizing the property of many

urban blacks. Bulldozers flattened their homes, and officials forced residents to move into townships or homelands (Bantustans), where people were not permitted to leave or to buy land. The government moved other blacks, along

Trucks bulldozed District 6, a predominantly Coloured neighborhood in Cape Town, in 1967.

with Coloureds and Asians, into urban areas that were zoned according to racial category. Buffer zones separated white neighborhoods from nonwhite neighborhoods

The ANCYL responded to the apartheid laws by persuading the ANC to take a more aggressive stand. The ANCYL organized boycotts, strikes, and other forms of civil disobedience. With ANCYL prodding, the ANC was transformed from a forum for discussion into a political action group.

During this time, South Africans became more familiar with another political philosophy called Communism. In theory, Communists promote a system in which major industries and banks are owned by the government and every citizen within the system has equal access to goods and services. The South African Communist Party (SACP), consisting of mostly whites, formed an

earlier alliance with the ANC to counter apartheid. To the South African government, whose main goal was to preserve the status of Afrikaners and other whites in South African society, Communism posed a serious threat. The South African regime was

one of many governments around the world that feared the spread of Communism. In the wake of World War II, when several eastern European countries chose Communism, free-market nations went on alert and vowed to thwart further spreading. To

A police officer arrests a Coloured woman for breaking the pass laws in the 1950s. All nonwhites were required to carry passbooks, containing identification information, at all times or risk arrest.

Mayibuye Centre/U.W.C.

South Africans, the threat of Communism was particularly close to home, as nearby African nations emerged from the restraints of European colonial rule and considered establishing Communist governments. The struggle that developed between Communist and non-Communist countries became known as the cold war. South Africa used its anti-Communist stance to attract support and trade from other anti-Communist countries, such as the United States.

Within the cold war atmosphere, the South African government passed the Suppression of Communism Act. It not only prohibited Communist groups from meeting but also allowed officials to declare unlawful any organization or publication suspected of trying to undermine the government. Anyone considered a threat to government security could be forbidden from speaking in public, could be denied the ability to travel freely, and could be forced to resign from all societies and organizations. Groups or individuals advocating racial equality were also deemed "communist." Those arrested under

The passbook of Joseph Ngulutyana is opened to the index to show the extent of the information found inside. In the early 1960s, resistance groups burned passbooks to protest the pass laws.

Mayibuye Centre/U.W.C.

the act had no right of appeal. The government used the vaguely written law against black opposition groups and their leaders, attributing all arrests to the prevention of Communist activity.

The Abolition of Passes and Consolidation of Documents Act ironically required all black South Africans over the age of 16 to carry identity passes so the government could regulate the movement of blacks in cities and other areas restricted to whites. Persons not carrying a pass-

book were subject to immediate arrest and imprisonment.

NONWHITES RESIST
At a convention held in December 1951, the ANC passed a resolution calling on the government to overturn the pass laws and the Suppression of Communism Act, end the removal of blacks from urban areas, and stop efforts to place Coloureds on a separate voting roll. The government rejected the ANC's demands in June 1952. The ANC then

teamed up with the South African Indian Congress (SAIC) and a number of Coloured South Africans to launch the Defiance Campaign. Under the direction of Albert Luthuli, a Zulu chief and prominent ANC leader, activists staged nonviolent strikes, sit-ins, rallies, and marches to draw international attention to apartheid's unfairness. The ANC's goal was to win equal rights for nonwhites.

The two-year Defiance Campaign had mixed results. The government arrested ANC leaders and more than 8,500 protesters. It passed the Criminal Laws Amendment Act, which provided stiff penalties for people who broke even minor laws during a protest or who encouraged others to join in public demonstrations. Censorship of anti-apartheid views in

newspapers and other media became common. Yet during the same period membership in the ANC grew from about 7,000 to more than 100,000. In the words of Luthuli, the Defiance Campaign was "the turning point" in the anti-apartheid movement.

The UN watched these developments with unease. As an early critic of South Africa's policies, the UN conducted many investigations of human-rights abuses by the white government and appealed for an end to apartheid. Although the

On June 26, 1955, South Africans of all different backgrounds attended the Congress of the People in Kliptown, South Africa, to formulate a plan for a democratic nation.

Mayibuye Centre/U.W.C.

government ignored most of these actions, the UN did focus more international attention on the injustices of apartheid. Other countries and organizations around the world, however, were reluctant to speak out against the system. South Africa provided valuable mineral resources that modern industrial economies needed. Leaders of such countries—including the United States, Great Britain, and Japan—were too busy advancing their own economic interests to protest against South Africa's treatment of its nonwhite citizens.

Unified by the Defiance Campaign, South African anti-apartheid groups—including a group of English-speakers (whites, for the most part) called the Congress of Democrats—formed the Congress Alliance in 1955. The alliance's goal was to develop a united front against apartheid and to rally the international community behind its cause. The alliance held the Congress of the People at which more than 2,000 South Africans from all ethnic backgrounds wrote the Freedom Charter. This document outlined a plan for a nonracial, unified, and democratic South Africa.

STRENGTHENING APARTHEID

Despite the work of anti-apartheid groups, the government continued to expand its apartheid policies. The Reservation of Separate Amenities Act created separate public drinking fountains, beaches, restrooms, buses, and railway cars for whites and non-whites. The Bantu Education Act created separate, government-controlled schools for black and white students, guaranteeing that whites would receive a superior education.

Apartheid laws further chipped away at the rights of both nonwhite and white groups that appeared to be a threat to the government. Soon after the Nationalists took over, Asians lost their representation in Parliament. In 1956, the Industrial Conciliation Act, originally passed in 1924, was amended to allow the minister of labor to reserve work for people of a particular racial category. Implementation of the act reserved the best-paying, highest-skilled jobs in government and private industry for whites. In the late 1950s, after an extensive congressional dispute, the government took away the voting rights of Coloured South Africans living in the Cape Province. To do this, the act had to pass by a two-thirds majority vote in Parliament. Nationalists secured

A prominent leader of the ANC during the 1950s, Albert Luthuli spearheaded the Defiance Campaign and was elected president of the ANC in 1952. In the same year, the government exiled him. In 1960 he won the Nobel Peace Prize for his efforts to end apartheid.

Archive Photos/London Daily Express

Sophiatown, 1955

One of the most notorious forced removals of the black population occurred in Sophiatown, a suburb of Johannesburg that was home to many leading black musicians, journalists, writers, and politicians. In 1955 the government declared Sophiatown a white area and sent bulldozers to flatten residents' houses.

Inhabitants described being awakened before dawn by police officers banging on their doors. "Before we even had opened the front door, I just heard the hammer on the pillar of the verandah . . . a big sound that made me wonder if I was dying," recalled Jane Dakile, a teacher at St. Cyprian's Anglican School. "That sound went right through my heart and I will never forget it."

The policemen informed Dakile that she and her husband were being moved immediately. "We had to take everything and throw it outside. Imagine taking your washing, just as it is, a chair just as it is—that's how [they] removed [us]. . . . I felt such a pity for my husband because he had built that house with his . . . bare hands. That house was our one and only little kingdom." A truck transported Dakile, her husband, and baby daughter to a government compound. "It was not very nice. It was just bricks, very cold, with no middle doors, only the outside doors. The houses were put together like trains."

Government workers waited with dump trucks outside of Sophiatown to move inhabitants and their belongings to a government compound.

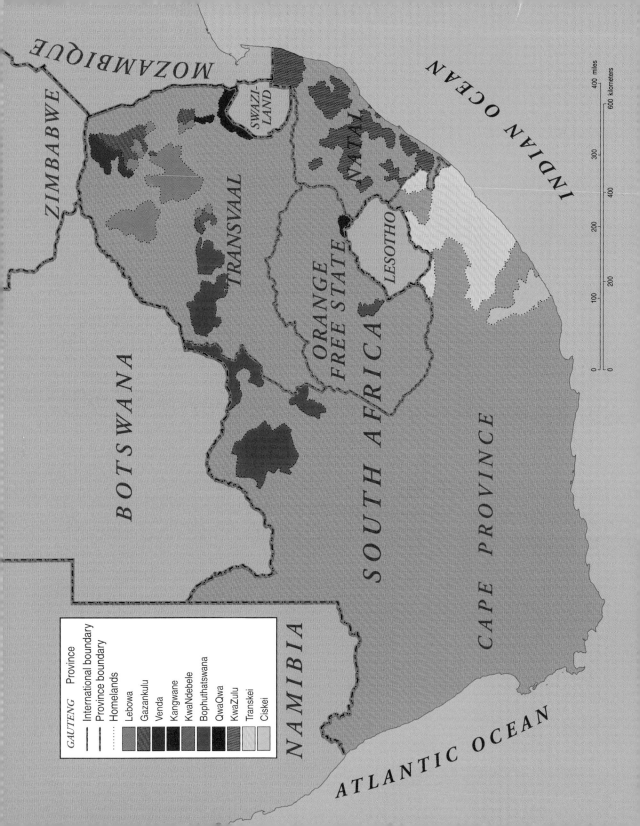

ZIMBABWE

MOZAMBIQUE

BOTSWANA

NAMIBIA

ATLANTIC OCEAN

INDIAN OCEAN

SOUTH AFRICA

CAPE PROVINCE

TRANSVAAL

ORANGE FREE STATE

NATAL

SWAZI-LAND

LESOTHO

GAUTENG Province
International boundary
Province boundary
Homelands

Lebowa
Gazankulu
Venda
Kangwane
KwaNdebele
Bophuthatswana
QwaQwa
KwaZulu
Transkei
Ciskei

400 miles

600 kilometers

400

300

200

100

400

200

200

100

0

0

Left: *The 10 former homelands consisted of many small land fragments located throughout the country. During apartheid, the government declared Bophuthatswana, Ciskei, Transkei, and Venda independent, although no other country in the world recognized them as such.*

the majority by creating additional senate seats for the sparsely populated rural areas of the Orange Free State, where mostly Afrikaners lived—those most likely to support the National Party.

Hendrik Verwoerd became president of South Africa in 1958. He believed further separation of South Africa's groups would strengthen the apartheid policy. In 1959 Parliament passed the Promotion of Bantu Self-Government Act, which recognized eight homelands as separate, self-governing nations. The government announced that since the black homelands would rule themselves, it was no longer necessary for black interests to be represented in the South African Parliament. (Later there were 10 homelands, where blacks were required by law to become citizens. While the South African government insisted that the homelands were self-governing nations, no other countries recognized them as such.)

On the surface, the Bantu Self Government Act appeared to give black South Africans independence from Afrikaner rule. But the homelands—located along South Africa's northern and eastern borders—were in the country's driest, most barren, and most remote areas, where the soil was too dry to support crops. The rest of South Africa contained the country's more fertile and mineral-rich lands and its most prosperous urban areas —such as Johannesburg and Cape Town. Most of the country's jobs were located outside the homelands.

ANC SPLITS

At the same time, an Africanist faction within the ANC was becoming disillusioned with the group's direction. Africanists promoted the idea of a solely black African state and objected to the ANC's cooperation with whites and Asians, whom they regarded as foreigners. Africanist ANC members also opposed the Freedom Charter. They distrusted the ANC's Communist members, whom Africanists felt were introducing a foreign ideology.

In April 1959, an Africanist minority, led by Robert Sobukwe, split from the ANC to form the Pan-Africanist Congress (PAC). In addition to their criticism of the ANC's multiracialism, the PAC's founders thought that the ANC was not aggressive enough in its efforts to end apartheid. They were

> *At the UN, South African Minister of Foreign Affairs Eric Louw justified the Bantu Self-Government Act. "The act . . . . follows recent trends and developments in the African continent and aims at progressively giving the Bantu control of his own homeland."*

Victims of the 1960 Sharpeville Massacre were left to lie in a street. The township's police chief said of the killings, "I don't know how many we shot, but if they do these things they must learn their lesson the hard way."

tired of the cautious approach to resistance and wanted to use violence to achieve their goals.

On March 21, 1960, the PAC launched a massive campaign to protest the pass laws. Thousands of demonstrators gathered in the black township of Sharpeville, in southern Transvaal Province, and marched toward police headquarters, where they planned to be arrested for not carrying their passbooks. Instead of arresting the activists, South African police fired into the crowd, killing 69 and injuring 180.

The events at Sharpeville made more people around the world aware of apartheid and of the South African government's willingness to use any means to maintain the policy. The ANC responded to Sharpeville by organizing a general labor strike that hampered the country's economy for three weeks. Then the ANC went one step further by declaring its willingness to use violence to fight apartheid laws.

In 1961 the ANC formed a military wing called Umkhonto we Sizwe (Spear of the Nation), commanded by Nelson Mandela. The group asserted its new stance: "The government has interpreted the peacefulness of the [ANC] movement as weakness. . . . Refusal to resort to force has been interpreted as an invitation to use armed force against the people without any fear of reprisals. The methods of Umkhonto we Sizwe mark a break with that past." The government

Archive Photos

responded to the creation of Umkhonto we Sizwe by declaring a state of emergency, by banning all black political organizations—including the ANC and the PAC—and by aggressively pursuing leaders of the two groups.

BREAK FROM BRITAIN

While Umkhonto we Sizwe was carrying out its guerrilla attacks, the South African government submitted an application for continued membership in the Commonwealth as an independent country. Nonwhite Commonwealth members, critical of South Africa's internal policies, threatened to leave if South Africa remained part of the organization. Verwoerd immediately withdrew his country's application and founded the Republic of South Africa. Withdrawal from the Commonwealth was one of the first big steps South Africa took toward isolation from the rest of the world. (Government structure in the Republic of South Africa remained the same. The governor general's title was changed to prime minister.)

By the 1960s, South Africa had become an unusually brutal police state. In 1962 the newly independent republic again took advantage of the widespread fear of Communism to pass the Sabotage Act.

TREASON TRIAL

The ACCUSED

DECEMBER 1956

Mayibuye Centre/U.W.C.

Showing an upbeat attitude, the 156 ANC leaders who were arrested and charged with treason under the Suppression of Communism Act posed before their trial began in 1956. The proceedings ended in 1961, when the court acquitted the last defendant.

The new law strengthened restrictions established under the Suppression of Communism Act, enabling South Africa's police to immediately detain Nelson Mandela, Walter Sisulu, and other high-ranking ANC leaders.

The international community began to pressure South Africa to abolish the apartheid system. In November 1962, for example, the UN General Assembly established the Special Committee Against Apartheid, which recommended that member-states sever all political and economic ties with South Africa.

The South African government ignored international actions and passed the Ninety-day Act, which gave police the power to jail people for 90 days without an arrest warrant. In the succeeding years, government officials continuously arrested, released, and re-arrested black, white, Coloured, and Asian political activists. Many spent months or years in jail. Others died after being tortured while in police custody.

In 1964 after a trial lasting more than two years, ANC leaders Nelson Mandela and Walter Sisulu were convicted of treason and sentenced to life imprisonment. At Mandela's sentencing, he addressed the courtroom. "During my lifetime I have fought against white domination and I have fought against black domination," he said. "I have cherished the ideal of a democratic and free society in which all persons will live together in harmony and with equal

> "During my lifetime I have fought against white domination and I have fought against black domination," Mandela said. "I have cherished the ideal of a democratic and free society in which all persons will live together in harmony and with equal opportunities. It is an ideal which I hope to live for and to achieve. But, if need be, it is an ideal for which I am prepared to die."

opportunities. It is an ideal which I hope to live for and to achieve. But, if need be, it is an ideal for which I am prepared to die."

OPPOSITION AT HOME

During Mandela's years in prison, his wife Winnie continued his struggle against apartheid, becoming a national symbol of defiance.

Meanwhile, Oliver Tambo, the only high-ranking ANC leader not in prison, left South Africa to establish an external wing of the organization. Within South Africa, the illegal ANC went underground, working secretly to resist apartheid.

In June 1964, the UN again issued a resolution condemning apartheid and began to explore the possibility of **economic sanctions** against South Africa. Although they complied with the arms embargo, powerful developed countries like the United States, Great Britain, and Japan felt South Africa provided too many of the mineral resources used in manufacturing to be easily ignored in trade circles. In addition, the United States excused many of the

apartheid policies as South Africa's way of suppressing Communism.

But other international organizations took stands against apartheid. Members of the World Health Organization (WHO), a specialized agency of the UN dedicated to improving people's health around the world, increasingly attacked South African policies. South Africa responded by leaving the organization in 1965. Amnesty International, a human rights organization, also began to actively follow events in South Africa. The group issued regular reports on the treatment of political dissidents in South Africa that revealed the brutality of the South African government.

During the late 1960s and 1970s, the South African government moved aggressively to segregate the nation's Coloured and Asian populations. A redefined classification policy based racial category not solely on appearance but also on proof of parentage and acceptance within the community. For example, persons wanting to be classified as white had to document their white parents and show that the white

Coloured Upheaval

In an article in the *Wall Street Journal,* Vincent Kolbe, a Coloured resident of District 6, described how his family was split apart by forced relocation. Unable to bear the hardship of living in a remote, marshy area known as the Cape Flats, his wife took advantage of her white, European facial features to keep her home.

"My wife became white," Kolbe said. "I don't blame her; she would have never made it in the townships. So we divorced. . . . It happened in many families. It was the price you paid for being colored." Kolbe settled in the Coloured township.

community welcomed them. The new classification policy forced Coloureds to move from their urban homes to segregated townships. Some Coloured communities were hit especially hard. In 1967 a part of Cape Town known as District 6, where mostly Coloured families had lived since 1834, was set aside for whites only. Giving only a few hours' notice, the government uprooted Coloured families and moved them to distant townships far from the city and their jobs.

The same fate befell Asians living in the city of Durban, which was once predominantly populated by people whose ancestors were from India. When the area was zoned for whites only in 1968, thousands of Indians

lost their jobs and businesses and ended up in crowded rural villages. Two, three, or four families often had to share one dwelling. Other families had to live in garages or backyard sheds.

In the late 1960s, young black university students in South Africa developed the Black Consciousness Movement (BCM) to fill the leadership void left by the banned ANC and PAC. Steve Biko, one of the BCM leaders, encouraged blacks to become more politically aware. Biko strongly believed that social justice in South Africa was not possible without majority rule. He urged blacks, Asians, and Coloureds to be proud of their respective heritages and to not rely on whites to solve their

Mbuyiselo Makhatsu carries the body of Hector Peterson, as Hector's sister, Antoinette, runs alongside. Hector was the first casualty in the Soweto uprising of 1976.

Maryibuye Centre/U.W.C.

political and economic problems. Many Asian and Coloured people began to identify more with blacks and the anti-apartheid movement as a result of the BCM.

Because of laws that had just been passed, much of the BCM's support came from the townships. One of the larger black townships was Soweto (South West Township), located just outside Johannesburg. In 1976 a new law required classes in Soweto to be taught in both English and Afrikaans. To the people of Soweto, Afrikaans was the language of apartheid and a symbol of oppression. About 10,000 students, many of them BCM supporters, staged demonstrations, marches, and boycotts to protest the language requirement.

Although the government later reversed its decision, the confrontation tapped into deep anger among young blacks. Violence erupted throughout South Africa in the following months, as rioting, arson, and killings spread to other black areas and to the Coloured population. When the spurt of violence ended, almost 500 people were dead. The government banned the BCM and all outdoor meetings of black groups.

OUTSIDERS TAKE ACTION

Events in South Africa were also raising the awareness of students and other groups outside the country. In the early 1970s, students in Boston, Massachusetts, picketed the main office of Polaroid, which made the passbooks required for all nonwhite South Africans. Polaroid officials responded by restricting sales to South Africa and by requiring South African Polaroid distributors to dramatically improve the salaries and benefits of nonwhite employees. Students at other U.S. colleges and universities set up mock shantytowns to protest their universities' financial holdings in South Africa.

Reverend Desmond Tutu, an Anglican minister in Soweto who was also general secretary of the South African Council of Churches (SACC), focused international attention on the inhumanity of apartheid and encouraged other countries to pressure the South African government to change. Some U.S. political leaders responded. They urged the U.S. government to put pressure on South

Churches Get Involved

Many of South Africa's religious congregations took a strong and early stand against apartheid. The government arrested or killed some priests and ministers for their resistance. After the Defiance Campaign of 1952, church leaders from around the world, including groups from the Church of England and the World Council of Churches, condemned apartheid. The 1960 Sharpeville Massacre helped more religious organizations within and outside of South Africa band together to oppose apartheid.

In the early 1980s, the Methodist Church, South Africa's second largest religious organization, condemned apartheid and publicly pledged to oppose the system. The Presbyterian Church, another major religious force in South Africa, encouraged ministers to break certain apartheid laws, including those prohibiting its clergy to perform marriage ceremonies for mixed-race couples.

Desmond Tutu, a black minister in the Anglican Church, won the respect and admiration of people around the world for his efforts to gain black civil rights in the 1960s and 1970s. In recognition of his work to peacefully end apartheid, Tutu won the Nobel Peace Prize in 1984.

Other churches were slower to join the struggle, because their leaders were concerned about mixing religion and politics. The Dutch Reformed Church actually promoted apartheid by maintaining separate churches for black, white, Asian, and Coloured members, claiming that the Bible endorsed this practice.

UPI/Corbis-Bettmann

Student demonstrators marched around an administration building at Harvard University in April 1978 to protest Harvard's refusal to sell off stocks held in companies operating in South Africa.

Africa to reform or to abolish apartheid. Several U.S. congresspeople and senators asked for economic sanctions against South Africa.

At the same time, local and regional governments in the United States took action. In December 1976, Madison, Wisconsin, became the first U.S. capital city to give preferential treatment to U.S. companies that did not have South African ties. Madison set a trend among local governments.

As the anti-apartheid movement in the United States grew, many leading U.S. companies reconsidered their presence in South Africa. In 1977 Leon Sullivan, a civil rights activist and director of General Motors, encouraged U.S. companies doing business with South Africa to follow a set of guidelines. About 170 out of the 350 corporations with operations in South Africa—including IBM, General Motors, Mobil, 3M, Citicorp, and Ford—adhered to the Sullivan Principles by promising to provide nonsegregated facilities, equal pay, and equal job opportunities for all of their South African employees, regardless of eth-

SOUTH AFRICA *Nation in Transition*

nic background. Polaroid went one step further and became the first U.S. company to withdraw from South Africa altogether. The Sullivan Principles, however, did little to push the government to end apartheid, so Sullivan later urged U.S. companies to completely stop doing business in South Africa. All 170 businesses eventually shut down their South African operations.

Meanwhile, on August 18, 1977, the BCM leader Steve Biko was arrested under an antiterrorism law and died less than one month later, while in police custody. The police initially claimed that Biko had starved himself. When an investigation revealed extensive brain damage, the police changed their story, stating that Biko had banged his head against a concrete wall until he passed out and later died. At the time, few blacks or whites believed the story.

Biko's death attracted worldwide media attention. U.S. President Jimmy Carter announced a mandatory arms embargo and voluntary economic sanctions. In February 1978, Citicorp, one of the largest banks in the United

Nonwhites would sometimes break petty apartheid laws as a form of protest. If this man had been caught sitting on a bench reserved for Europeans, he would have faced a $20 fine or 20 days in prison.

At the time of his death, Steve Biko had become very popular with young black South Africans.

States, refused to make any more loans to South Africa. Other investors, including U.S. universities and British and Scandinavian companies, also withdrew their support.

THE TURBULENT 1980s

During the 1980s, a change in the political environment in the United States and Great Britain had a dramatic impact on the South African economy. U.S. President Ronald Reagan revived the Communist threat, pushed for friendship with South Africa, and took a stance against sanctions. He also acknowledged that South African soil held much needed minerals. The new conservative prime minister of Great Britain, Margaret Thatcher, shared Reagan's views. When gold prices shot up in the early 1980s, South Africa's economy boomed, enabling the government to dodge the effects of those sanctions that were still being enforced.

In 1983 a new constitution restored voting rights to Asians and Coloureds and established Coloured and Asian legislative chambers in Parliament. (Blacks were still excluded.) Leaders hoped the constitution would alienate Coloureds and Indians from blacks. Banned BCM leaders responded by organizing a campaign of protests and strikes. The government declared a **state of emergency** and police arrested and imprisoned more than 30,000 black South Africans. Journalists were forbidden to report what had happened. By the end of the year, police had arrested almost 300,000 people for breaking the pass laws, more than 100,000 people for trespassing, and 11,000 people for violating curfew. The crackdown failed to end the protests, and international outrage at

Police attempted to control students in a Johannesburg anti-apartheid march in 1986. Under the apartheid regime, the police often arrested people for petty offenses, such as trespassing and breaking curfew, to contain anti-apartheid activities.

Hundreds of black miners protest unsafe working conditions at a memorial service for the victims of South Africa's worst gold mine accident, in which 177 employees died in an underground fire.

the government's behavior increased.

In 1984 the price of gold plummeted, drought struck, and the level of black resistance in the townships continued to climb. South Africa found itself in serious political and economic trouble and in need of outside investment. The government felt forced to make reforms. After P.W. Botha was elected president of South Africa later that year, the government changed some minor apartheid laws. Over the objections of 18 high-ranking Afrikaners who had joined the Conservative Party, the Botha government desegregated some hotels, restaurants, trains, buses, and public facilities.

Botha hoped these reforms would calm nonwhites by giving them a greater opportunity to participate in South African society, while still maintaining white supremacy. But Botha's reforms had just the opposite effect. Although rioting in Coloured and Asian areas died down when parliamentary elections were held in August 1984 (most Coloured and Indians boycotted the elections), violence in black areas reached an all-time high on the twenty-fifth anniversary of the Sharpeville massacre. By the end of 1984, more than 175 people, mostly blacks, had died in the protests.

Labor strikes, bus and school boycotts, and clashes between township residents and police continued into 1985, when political violence left almost 900 more South Africans dead. The government responded by calling another state of emergency, which gave police almost unlimited powers. Rather than ending the resistance movement, the government's response only strengthened national opposition to apartheid. International pressure also went up a notch. Chase Manhattan Bank, one of South Africa's largest lenders, pulled out of the country. Other U.S. and European banks followed their lead. The Commonwealth heads of government drafted an accord demanding that South Africa release Nelson Mandela, lift the ban on opposition groups, and dismantle the entire apartheid

making new investments in South Africa, stopped South African Airlines from landing in the United States, and banned a long list of South African imports. Many U.S. companies with operations in South Africa pulled out of the country.

The sanctions soon began to hurt South Africa's economy. More money had been spent to keep apartheid alive, leaving little left over to spend on areas such as job creation, health care, and education.

Between 1985 and 1990, almost 170 U.S. companies, including Pan Am, Uniroyal, and IBM, left South Africa. Economists estimate that South Africa lost more than 250,000 jobs and about $10 billion due to U.S. sanctions.

---

system. Great Britain and other Commonwealth countries also imposed sanctions. Because Britain accounted for a substantial amount of South Africa's foreign investment, this was a considerable blow to the South African economy.

In 1986, over Reagan's objections, the U.S. Congress passed the Comprehensive Anti-Apartheid Act. It prohibited U.S. companies from

Estimates suggest that international economic sanctions cost the South African economy more than $40 billion. Botha's government was forced to take action. Parliament abolished the pass laws, the Prohibition of Mixed Marriages Act, the job reservation laws, and the ban on nonwhite trade unions. Botha also lifted the state of emergency that had been enforced since mid-1985.

VIOLENCE RAGES ON

But black South Africans didn't think Botha's government went far enough. The most restrictive and oppressive apartheid laws—the Group Areas Act, the Population Registration Act, and the 1913 land act—were still in place. The government continued to maintain a racially segregated education system and to spend far more on the education of white children than on the teaching of blacks, Coloureds, and Asians. Black health and welfare services were far inferior to services for whites, if they existed at all. Most blacks remained poor and unemployed. Perhaps more important, blacks still lacked the right to vote.

Civil unrest in black townships pushed the government to declare another state of emergency in 1986. Other forms of protest continued to erupt throughout the country. In 1987 alone, unionized black workers organized more than 1,000 strikes against unequal pay and hazardous working conditions in South Africa's gold and diamond mines. Although still banned by the government, the under-

To stop the demolition of squatter shacks in Soweto, these young South Africans set fire to cars in the township in July 1990. Police broke up the demonstration by firing tear gas into the crowd.

ground ANC stepped up its campaign of sabotage by bombing restaurants, shopping centers, and sports areas in South African cities.

The government responded by banning the United Democratic Front (UDF), the largest anti-apartheid group in the country. The government also refused to grant voting rights to the black majority and tried to pass legislation to heavily penalize violations of the Group Ar-

eas Act. Both the Coloured and Asian chambers blocked the legislation.

To quiet the storm of protests at these actions, Botha agreed to release Mandela if the ANC would renounce violence as a weapon against apartheid. Mandela refused. Unwilling to weaken his government's monopoly on power, Botha was not prepared to go any further. In August 1989 after suffering a stroke, Botha resigned, and

education minister F.W. de Klerk became president of South Africa.

Considered the most conservative of Botha's possible successors, de Klerk shocked South Africans in his speech on the opening of Parliament in February 1990. He announced plans to release Nelson Mandela; to legalize the ANC, the PAC, the SACP, and the UDF; and to dismantle what remained of the apartheid system.⊕

CHAPTER

4

THE PRESENT CONFLICT

The election of 1989 marked a turning point in South African history. By the time F.W. de Klerk clarified his intention to end apartheid, an increasing number of whites had grown weary of the fighting and of the impact of political and economic sanctions. De Klerk and several others in the National Party realized that the only way to prevent further economic deterioration and civil unrest was to transfer power to South Africa's black majority and hope to preserve for whites as many advantages as possible.

In 1990 de Klerk called for the creation of a new South Africa. "It is time for us to break out of the cycle of violence and break through to peace and reconciliation," he said. "The time for negotiation has arrived." De Klerk lifted the ban on the 33 remaining opposition groups. On February 11, 1990, he released 30 ANC leaders, including Nelson Mandela, who had spent 27 years in prison. Black South Africans across the country celebrated the news.

De Klerk repealed the Separate Amenities Act. Aside from a few angry demonstrations staged by Afrikaners, all ethnic groups began to use the same facili-

South Africans in Johannesburg celebrated Mandela's 1990 release from Robben Island near Cape Town, where he spent 18 of his 27 years in prison.

ties peacefully. In 1991, de Klerk abolished the Group Areas Act and the Population Registration Act. Countries began to lift sanctions.

Meanwhile the ANC restructured and prepared for government negotiations. Conflicts between supporters with different ideologies, however, made restructuring difficult. While Mandela hoped to work with de Klerk's National Party and others to create a multiparty democracy, other ANC supporters, including Winnie Mandela, thought he was compromising too much. Winnie Mandela held significant power among the more radical ANC factions and indicated that her husband might not be defending black interests strongly enough. Her influence weakened in 1992, when she was convicted for her involvement in the kidnapping of four young black activists and the murder of one of them. The Mandelas separated and later divorced, and Nelson eliminated Winnie from all offices within the ANC.

PROLONGED NEGOTIATIONS
In the early 1990s ANC leaders met several times

> *"It is time for us to break out of the cycle of violence and break through to peace and reconciliation,"* de Klerk said. *"The time for negotiation has arrived."*

with de Klerk, government representatives, and other political groups to discuss the transfer of power to the black majority. Twice the ANC withdrew from talks because of IFP attacks against the ANC, which, despite pleas from Mandela and other ANC leaders, the government did nothing to discourage or prevent. At the time, the ANC began to suspect that a third group, possibly the government-sponsored police force, was involved in the IFP attacks. These suspicions were validated when the international media reported that the South African government had made secret payments to the IFP, supplied it with arms, and provided it with military training. Nations around the world expressed their loss of faith in the de Klerk regime.

Other problems suspended the talks. Fearing that blacks might take re-

venge against whites, the Nationalists vigorously fought for the power to veto (overrule) decisions made by a black-majority government. This was unacceptable to the ANC, which organized strikes and other nonviolent protests to force the government to change its position.

Worried that violence would abort the peace process, a group of businessmen and church leaders met to come up with a plan. After listening to the ideas of political and community leaders, they introduced the National Peace Accord in September 1991. The accord was a pact signed by 26 representatives from the major political parties and organizations, the homelands, and the trade unions, to do whatever they could to end violence. Most important, the accord established a network of peace organizations located throughout the country that provided a forum for the resolution of

In March 1992, a student supporter of F.W. de Klerk campaigned at school for a "Yes" vote to de Klerk's proposed reforms.

The Conservative Party refused to participate in CODESA. Seventeen former National Party members joined the Conservative Party when de Klerk began reforms. Some conservatives, including former president P. W. Botha, branded de Klerk a traitor for dismantling the apartheid system. In March 1992, de Klerk held a special election to give all whites a chance to voice their opinions on extending voting rights to blacks. More than two-thirds of those voting approved of de Klerk's agenda.

political and community conflicts. Many speculate that without the National Peace Accord, free elections would not have been possible.

Under the Peace Accord, negotiations began to improve. The multiparty Convention for a Democratic South Africa (CODESA) met for the first time in December 1991. Representatives from the government, the ANC, the IFP, the homelands, and 19 other political groups attended the meeting. But dissension still stalled

progress. The IFP withdrew shortly after the talks began, when Buthelezi failed to win extra delegates for the Zulu monarchy. Negotiations became deadlocked when the government's representatives again pushed for veto rights over black-majority decisions.

While talks were delayed, de Klerk and Mandela continued to meet. On September 20, 1992, they signed the Record of Understanding in which the government agreed to protect the ANC from IFP attacks.

In early April 1993, talks to draft an interim constitution resumed, but another high-profile murder threatened hopes for a peaceful transition. A member of a white-extremist group murdered Chris Hani, the popular army commissioner of Umkhonto we Sizwe and Mandela's possible successor. An explosive outpouring of anti-white sentiment followed Hani's murder. Extremists rioted and committed other random violence. Despite Mandela's request for South Africans to remain calm, protesters looted stores and set fire to vehicles. Supporters of the PAC whipped up black frustrations with their motto: "One Settler, One Bullet." As the violence escalated, a group of blacks killed three whites in a black township near Cape Town, and a white group killed two more blacks in Vanderbijlpark, a city just south of Johannesburg. On July 25, 1993, black extremists used automatic rifles and hand grenades to kill or wound 50 whites who were worshiping at a Cape Town church.

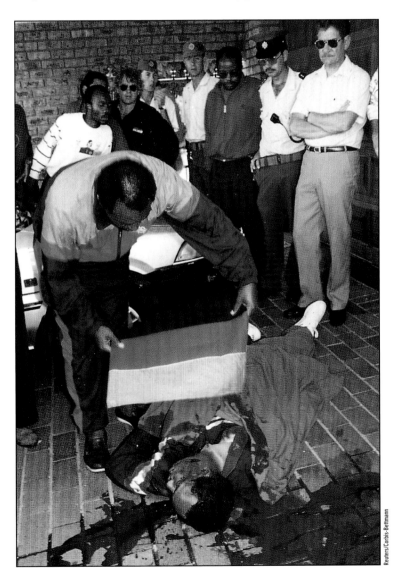

Reuters/Corbis-Bettmann

BREAKTHROUGH

Despite the setbacks, Mandela and de Klerk held steady in their resolve to frame a peaceful transition to democracy. Their work resulted in an interim constitution that was formally approved by the South African Parliament on November 22, 1993. After all sides agreed to compromise, negotiators for the government, the ANC, and the IFP pledged to support a nonracial, nonsexist, unified, and democratic South Africa based on the principle of "one person, one vote." While minority political parties would be guaranteed a

ANC leader Tokyo Sexwale covered Chris Hani's body with an ANC flag shortly after Hani was murdered in front of his suburban Johannesburg home. Many viewed Hani as Mandela's successor to the ANC leadership.

De Klerk and Mandela walked together to give a joint statement in May 1990 about the progress of negotiations between the South African government and the ANC.

Archive Photos/Uli Michel/Reuters

until a permanent constitution came into force.

The new constitution also changed South Africa's political boundaries. The country's four provinces and ten black homelands were replaced by nine provinces. Drafters of the interim constitution hoped that these new provincial lines would help to unify the country by removing historic and geographic barriers between whites and nonwhites.

FEAR OF CHANGE

Not all South Africans welcomed the country's transition to democracy. Many whites feared a civil war would erupt when blacks gained political control. In 1993 more than 8,000 people—most of them white—left South Africa. Although 8,000 may not appear to be a

voice in the new government, they would not be able to veto the majority's will. The interim constitution outlawed racial and other types of discrimination and declared all South Africans to be equal under the law.

Negotiators agreed to hold the first multiracial elections in South Africa's history in April 1994. Parliament created the Transitional Executive Council (TEC), consisting of representatives of the ANC, the National Party, and 14 other ethnically diverse groups, to supervise the elections, which would put in place new national and provincial governments. The nation's new interim constitution would go into effect immediately after the election and would remain active

Right: Apartheid went beyond South Africa's borders. The South African government's control over and raids into Namibia beginning in 1916 caused international outcry until South Africa finally withdrew from the country in 1990.

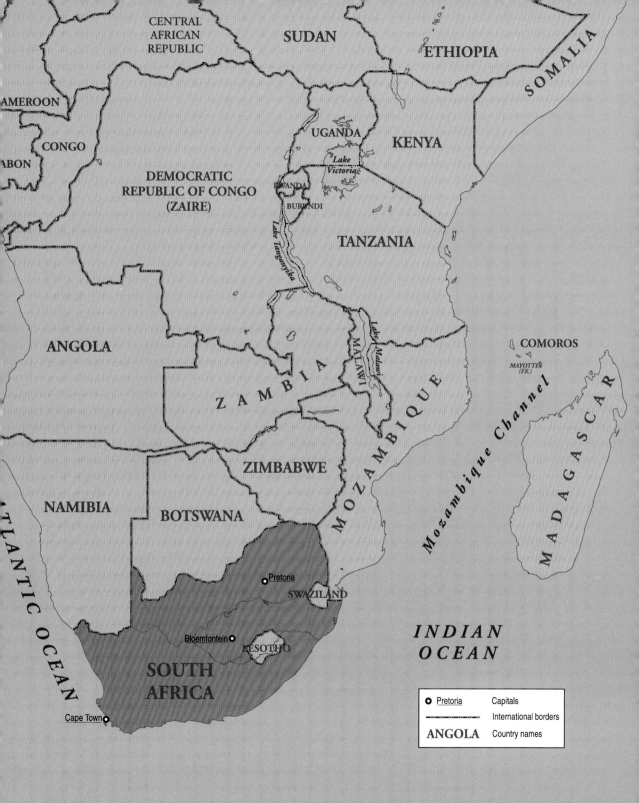

CENTRAL
AFRICAN
REPUBLIC

SUDAN

ETHIOPIA

SOMALIA

CAMEROON

CONGO

GABON

DEMOCRATIC
REPUBLIC OF CONGO
(ZAIRE)

UGANDA

Lake Victoria

KENYA

RWANDA

BURUNDI

TANZANIA

Lake Tanganyika

ANGOLA

Z A M B I A

MALAWI

Lake Malawi

COMOROS

MAYOTTE (FR.)

M O Z A M B I Q U E

Mozambique Channel

M A D A G A S C A R

ZIMBABWE

NAMIBIA

BOTSWANA

SOUTH
AFRICA

Pretoria

SWAZILAND

Bloemfontein

LESOTHO

Cape Town

A T L A N T I C   O C E A N

*INDIAN
OCEAN*

○ Pretoria	Capitals
	International borders
ANGOLA	Country names

significant number, the whites who could afford to leave—young professionals and wealthy older people—would have helped the new government rebuild the economy. Most of the whites who planned to stay were conservative Afrikaners who couldn't afford to—and didn't wish to—move because their only ties were to South Africa.

As election day neared, many conservative whites prepared for the worst. Fearing a civil war and power outages, people waited in lines outside of grocery stores to stock up on canned food, candles, and ammunition. Other white South Africans made plans to be out of the country at voting time. Listeners called in to radio talk shows for information about obtaining visas and leaving the country. About 10,000 wealthy whites left South Africa during the elections to vacation in Zimbabwe.

Meanwhile, extremist groups exploited divisions between white South Africans and black South Africans. White supremacist groups—such as the Afrikaner Resistance Movement, the White Liberation Movement, and the Boer Resistance Movement—openly opposed government reforms. These organizations bombed ANC offices and businesses owned by local officials sympathetic to the ANC. The groups targeted railroad tracks and electrical pylons in the Orange Free State and western Transvaal and later briefly occupied the World Trade Center in Johannesburg, where government and anti-apartheid delegates had

In the township of Boipatong, 40 miles south of Johannesburg, IFP members allegedly arrived in marked police cars and killed about 39 ANC supporters. De Klerk denounced the killings and traveled to the township to offer his condolences to the villagers. A group of about 3,000 angry protesters met him, shouting "go away, murderer!" After de Klerk left the scene, police opened fire on the crowd, killing at least 3 and injuring more than 20. The killings attracted international attention and prompted the UN to launch an investigation.

AP/Wide World Photos

Police and residents watched as a coroner prepared to move a victim of the Biopatong Massacre.

South Africans formed spiraling lines outside the polling station in the black township of Soweto on Wednesday, April 27, 1994. A majority of South Africa's 22 million voters cast ballots in the country's first all-race elections.

gathered for negotiations. Members of the Afrikaner Resistance Movement spray-painted angry slogans on the negotiating room walls and verbally abused the delegates. Many in South Africa and around the world denounced the extremists' actions.

The IFP, concerned that its interests in self-rule would not be represented in a government dominated by the ANC, also stirred unrest by threatening to boycott the elections and continued its campaign of violence against ANC supporters. One night in February 1994, for example, IFP members or police imposters surrounded and shot 15 sleeping teenagers who were campaigning for the ANC in the village of Mahlele in southern present-day KwaZulu-Natal.

ELECTION AND REFORM

In spite of these setbacks and scares, millions of South Africans peacefully voted in their country's first national, nonracial election. Many had waited for hours in long lines, eager to participate in choosing their country's new leaders. Election observers were impressed by the huge turnout, which they estimated at 86 percent of

South Africa's 23 million eligible voters. The lack of violent incidents also relieved observers.

Even before half of the votes were counted, de Klerk conceded defeat. Mandela had won almost 63 percent of the vote to become the new president of South Africa. People around the world tuned in to watch South Africans of all ethnic groups unite in the streets of Johannesburg to celebrate.

Based on the election results, the National Party had won 22 percent of the vote, and the IFP had won 10 percent. Both had earned a voice in the new government. De Klerk, the last president under the apartheid system and a member of the National Party, became deputy president of South Africa. Buthelezi, head of the IFP, became a cabinet minister.

The ANC, the National Party, the IFP, and some smaller parties agreed to form a **coalition** government in the interests of national unity and stability. The new government, called the Government of National Unity (GNU), consisted of a multiparty and multiracial cabinet that made decisions at

During a peace march in Durban, a Zulu teenager used a knobkerrie (a traditional Zulu club) to knock down a de Klerk campaign poster.

the national, provincial, and local levels. The three parties successfully cooperated on most issues and made decisions by **consensus.**

The coalition government developed a blueprint for reform. Through the Reconstruction and Development Program (RDP), the government unveiled plans to equip rural homes with electricity and indoor plumbing; to redistribute land; to reduce crime; and to build new homes, schools, and hospitals.

The government also intended to create 2.5 million new jobs and to pass laws that provided better job opportunities for nonwhites in government and private industry. Workplaces opened up to people of all races and backgrounds, and, as a result, the economic status of blacks began to show small signs of improvement. The black middle-class, for example, which had once made up only a tiny fraction of the population, rose to more than a million.

> *Before South Africa's first democratic elections, the United Nations sent more than 2,500 observers. They verified that the voting process was free, fair, and proceeded in an orderly manner.*

The government's land-reform proposal had two parts: redistribution and restitution. Under land redistribution, blacks would be given back land or would be compensated for land that was taken away from 1913 onward. Blacks would also be permitted to buy public and private land and would be given more secure rights to lands that they occupy. The purpose of restitution is to compensate those who have suffered as a direct result of the forced-removal policy.

TRUTH AND RECONCILIATION

In July 1995, Mandela established the Truth and Reconciliation Commission (TRC). Made up of people from different socioeconomic and ethnic groups, the commission provided a forum in which victims and oppressors were free to tell their stories to make peace with their past. In December 1995, Archbishop Tutu was appointed to head the commission. To speed the nation's healing process, the TRC announced that those who came forward to publicly confess their involvement in terrorism, torture, or other political crimes during apartheid could avoid

Mandela shares a light-hearted moment with his cabinet minister, Mangosuthu Buthelezi, head of the IFP. Their relationship has not been easy. In early 1997, Mandela worked to gain Buthelezi's trust by appointing him acting president while Mandela was out of the country.

prosecution by applying for **amnesty.** To be granted amnesty, the perpetrator was required to fully disclose what had happened, tell why he or she had committed the crime, and show how the act had conformed to official policy at the time. Amnesty applicants were not required to apologize or to show remorse for what they had done. The commission felt that they had made major breakthroughs in exposing the truths of the apartheid era when, on January 28, 1997, five former security policemen confessed to the killing of Steve Biko in 1977. In July, four PAC members admitted that they had killed Amy Biehl, a 26-year-old American Fulbright scholar who was in South Africa in 1993 to help register voters for the first all-race elections. And in August, the two men

convicted of killing Chris Hani applied for amnesty.

Although the commission hoped such confessions would lead to forgiveness and reconciliation, many victims, such as Ntsiki Biko and Hani's family, wanted the perpetrators to be severely punished. Family members weren't the only ones calling

for justice. Demonstrators marched outside the Hani hearings holding signs that read, "Murderers Belong in Jail." Other victims, did not call for punishment—they just wanted it to be known that they had suffered. Some were even willing to forgive.

When hearings first began, most of those who told their

In recognition of their success in negotiating a peaceful transition from apartheid to political democracy, de Klerk and Mandela were awarded a joint Nobel Peace Prize in 1993.

Reuters/Corbis-Bettmann

On April 15, 1996—the first day of Truth and Reconciliation hearings—Archbishop Desmond Tutu and the other commissioners listened to testimony about apartheid-era human rights abuses.

stories to the commission had been victims; few perpetrators came forward. Many whites objected to the hearings, complaining that the commission was a waste of the taxpayer's money. Others called the hearings a "witch hunt" that unfairly targeted whites who had simply fought to defend their country. In May 1997, F.W. de Klerk withdrew the National Party's cooperation from the hearings, claiming that the commission was biased. De Klerk had been

pressured to testify before the commission about his involvement in and knowledge of apartheid-era crimes, but he refused, denying that he knew of any abuses during his presidency. In August 1997, de Klerk retired from politics, claiming that he hoped to free the National Party from its past and to allow his fellow party members time to prepare for the 1999 elections.

During the same month, the Inkatha Freedom Party also criticized the commis-

sion for being biased and then withdrew from talks with the ANC aimed at ending political violence in KwaZulu-Natal. The IFP was angry over testimony that revealed its cooperation with the apartheid-era government. Witnesses provided evidence that the government had trained 200 IFP members in paramilitary tactics used to assassinate ANC leaders and to increase hostilities between black South Africans. The IFP stated,

Sports and Symbols

Rugby is one of the most popular sports among white South Africans, especially Afrikaners. Because rugby was seen as a primarily "white sport," blacks generally shunned South Africa's all-white national team, the Springboks.

After apartheid, Nelson Mandela saw an opportunity to use the sport's popularity among whites to help unify his country. Mandela showed his support in 1995, the year that the Springboks made it to the rugby World Cup finals, which were set to be played in Johannesburg. Before the World Cup matches began, Mandela urged blacks to rally be-

hind the national team. He even wore a green Springboks cap to black political meetings. "I told them, 'We wish our boys success,'" he later recalled in an interview with the *New York Times Magazine*, "and they would clap politely—not so enthusiastically."

Yet Mandela was undaunted. When the team beat the odds and made it to the finals, he showed up in the Springboks locker room before the game, sporting a green team jersey, to wish the players good luck. Mandela then joined thousands of his fellow fans in the stands, where he anxiously watched the Springboks battle to an edge-of-the-seat

During apartheid, white schools had first-rate sports grounds and equipment, while nonwhite schools didn't have money for basic supplies, such as textbooks and writing paper.

15–12 upset victory. When it was all over, Mandela, still wearing the green jersey, seized the moment. He walked out onto the field to present the trophy and was met by an Afrikaner crowd that roared its approval by chanting, "Nelson, Nelson, Nelson."

The unified crowd was a powerful gesture and symbol of reconciliation. "It [the event] had a devastating effect on the far-right white groups, the people who had refused to vote in 1994 or to recognize the new Constitution, saying 'It's not our country,'" noted an observer in the *New York Times Magazine*. "The groups simply disintegrated. Their people stopped using the symbols of the past, the old flag, the old songs. Mandela became the symbol of the whole country."

"The Truth Commission, flawed in every facet since its inception, merely creates an arena for biased propaganda and clichés of political correctness, which end up echoing what the witnesses think the inquisitors want to hear."

When the truth about apartheid atrocities unraveled, whites quieted down. Many who had voted the National Party into office again and again over the years had refused to believe news of killings and beatings of political dissidents. The stories that surfaced in hearings forced these people to confront the realities of the apartheid years. Gradually, more perpetrators came forward, but time was running out. The two years granted to the commission to hear all cases ended in December 1997. By mid 1997, only one former cabinet minister, Adriaan Vlok, who was minister of law and order from 1986 to 1991, had applied for amnesty. Commission members hope that future developments provide leads to other former high-ranking officials from the apartheid era. Only when the truth is known can South African society as a whole move on.

In the meantime, Mandela has extended his negotiating skills to other African nations to facilitate peaceful resolutions to age-old conflicts. In May 1997, he played an important part in attempting to bring about a relatively calm transfer of power in the Democratic Republic of Congo (formerly Zaire). Mandela's leadership and dedication to peaceful resolution have helped establish South Africa as a future leader on the African continent and in the world.

As South Africans plan for tomorrow, many wonder about what will happen when Mandela steps down from the presidency, as he plans to do in 1999. His ability to compromise, to see all

Thabo Mbeki was sworn in as first deputy president in May 1994. Mbeki shares Mandela's commitment to reconciliation and economic reform.

sides of an issue, and to negotiate have been indispensable in the transition from minority to majority rule. Mandela has handpicked South Africa's deputy president, Thabo Mbeki, as his successor. Mbeki, viewed as more of a deal-making businesslike leader than Mandela, may be just what South Africa needs to carry it into the next century. In any case, the fate of the nation rests in the hands of those who win the 1999 elections.

"We live with the hope that as she battles to remake herself, South Africa will be like a microcosm of the new world that is striving to be born."

CHAPTER 5
WHAT'S BEING DONE TO SOLVE THE PROBLEM

South Africans set aside March 21, 1995, to remember and to forgive. On this date, exactly 35 years after the Sharpeville massacre, people of all ethnic backgrounds gathered to commemorate what had become a national holiday. In the streets of Sharpeville, church leaders worshiped with some of the men and women who had been present at the original protest in 1960.

One of the speakers at the celebration was Willem Verwoerd, the grandson of Hendrik Verwoerd, the architect of apartheid and South Africa's prime minister at the time of the Sharpeville massacre. Willem Verwoerd had become a member of the ANC, and his wife was an ANC member of Parliament. In his remarks, Verwoerd described how he had broken with his family's past to join those who fought against apartheid.

The gathering demonstrated that South Africans are attempting to understand their past and to reconcile their differences. When apartheid was dismantled, South Africans faced a whole new set of challenges. To begin the process of building an economically strong democratic country, they had to accept their past and forgive those who had harmed them.

The main forum for such confessions and occasional apologies, where victims and oppressors told the truth about apartheid, were the TRC hearings, which brought many crimes out in the open. The commission hopes that when all South Africans know what happened to nonwhites and anti-apartheid activists, they will grow to better understand one another and move on to reform South Africa together.

HARD WORK AHEAD

If accepting the truth and granting forgiveness are the first steps, then creating an economy in which black, Coloured, and Asian people have the same opportunities as white people is next. Educational reforms play a large part in preparing nonwhites for the jobs available to them. Schools are being restructured to ensure that all students, regardless of color, have equal access to public education. The government has made plans to improve the training of black teachers and has promised each child up to six years of free education. A growing number of nonwhite students are attending urban colleges and universities that were once reserved only for whites.

Although the black majority runs the government, control of the country's economy remains firmly in the hands of white elites. Meanwhile, many black South Africans are unable to find jobs. With an estimated 400,000 new workers entering the job market each year and with few jobs to accommodate them, unemployment stands at around 40 percent.

This dismal picture looks bleaker when those seeking jobs go home. Many blacks still live in squatter communities where they have built makeshift homes out of scrap wood and cardboard. Sometimes, when squatters have settled on land that the government has designated for new homes, the government has forced occupants to resettle elsewhere. Rampant crime, a direct result of high unemployment, worsens conditions in poor areas, where residents are most vulnerable to random acts of violence. In contrast, many white urban South Africans have high standards of living. Although crime is an issue for all South Africans, whites can afford to hire security companies for protection and tend to live in relatively secure neighborhoods.

More foreign investment could address two of South Africa's toughest problems— high unemployment and soaring crime rates. The return of foreign companies could create more jobs, which would give more people a stake in South Africa's future. If people had a greater sense of hope, the crime rate might decrease. Many companies that left South Africa in the mid-1980s are still hesitant to return, however. They claim that the South African work force is unskilled, too expensive, and too political to warrant their investment. In trying to attract foreign investors, the government is in an awkward position. To create the calm climate investors look for, Mandela has attempted to suppress the strikes started by black workers who demand better wages and working conditions—the same blacks who are ardent supporters of the ANC. At a time when businesses can find skilled workers in Asia— where lower standards of

As the government builds new homes, it also upgrades older dwellings by installing electricity and plumbing. From the rural areas once set aside for blacks, many residents moved to the cities where overcrowding was already a problem.

living keep wages down and allow companies to save money—South Africa doesn't appear to be the best place to set up shop. Safety is also an issue. Robberies, burglaries, and carjackings make South Africa a risk.

Foreign businesses have had other problems in South Africa. Robert Newman of Jaerns Housing, Ltd., a prefabricated housing firm based in North Dakota, shared his company's experiences at a Minnesota conference. Although South Africa needs between 4 and 8 million housing units, mortgages are astronomically high, and the average black South African can't afford them. Yet Newman thinks South Africa has great potential. "Things will take time," he said, "but there is an aura of hope, and as long as people see progress, that is acceptable."

At the same conference, Dr. Brian Gould, of the United HealthCare Corporation, emphasized problems his company has had in South Africa with training employees and with boycotts by doctors. Gould's firm has made the decision to stay and resolve these issues. "We are committed to the long haul," he said, "but it has been a sobering experience."

THE GOVERNMENT PLAN

The new government enacted the RDP to address many of the issues that scare companies away. The hope is that when most South Africans have adequate housing, and are able to get a good education and decent job, the crime rate will decrease and South Africa will be a safer place to do business.

The core of South Africa's reform package is to provide the most basic needs first— building houses, hospitals, and roads; wiring rural

New roads will make travel easier in South Africa. During apartheid the government built and maintained good roads in white areas but neglected the dirt roads in the townships and homelands.

homes with electricity; and installing plumbing. But with progress, life becomes more complicated and more expensive. Homeowners with electricity and plumbing must pay electricity, water, and sewer bills. People with electricity are also likely to acquire modern conveniences—such as refrigerators and television sets. More people will need jobs to be able to pay for and enjoy the improvements.

Through the reform program, the government has also worked to bridge the income gap between black and white South Africans. The Johannesburg city government adopted a plan by which its revenues would be devoted disproportionately to serving and improving predominantly black living areas. Although whites challenged this plan in court, the courts upheld the plan in 1997.

The RDP requires companies to provide equal employment opportunities for all South Africans. To comply with these regulations, white business owners have hired black workers to fill positions for which they may or may not be qualified or trained. Although this may seem like a

MaryBaye Centre/UWC.

Robben Island

In many ways, South Africa has moved out of the shadows of its apartheid past. Robben Island, site of the prison where Nelson Mandela spent 18 of his 27 years in jail, was shut down in December 1996. These days visitors come from around the world, as well as South Africa, to see the tiny 6- by 9-foot cell where Mandela was confined. Humphrey Matyeka, a black resident of Johannesburg, his wife, and daughter were among the first to tour the prison when it opened to the public. "It's touching," Matyeka said, "to see this cell where Mandela lived all those years and still came out with so much grace, with no desire for revenge. How many of us could do that?"

big step forward, many blacks in this situation have become frustrated, because their white supervisors don't trust them with the responsibilities ordinarily assigned to a white holding the same job.

At the same time, non-blacks in South Africa feel that the new laws are unfair to white, Coloured, and Asian workers. Black workers counter that if they hadn't been denied a quality education, they would be qualified. They feel they should be given a chance to catch up with their white peers.

Winston Floquet, chief executive of Fleming Martin Securities, states the importance of education in economic development: "People say South Africa is going to be another tiger economy, like the ones in Asia. But you can't get there from such a low skills base. It will haunt us for at least another

"People say South Africa is going to be another tiger economy, like the ones in Asia. But you can't get there from such a low skills base. It will haunt us for at least another decade."

These students at the integrated University of the Witwatersrand will play an important part in South Africa's future. With a better educated workforce, South Africa will be more likely to attract the foreign investors necessary to improve the country's economy.

Some white South Africans are making an effort to learn about nonwhite cultures. These students at the University of the Witwatersrand in Johannesburg are studying the Zulu language. The university has offered African language courses since the 1970s, but registration increased only at the end of white-minority rule.

decade." The RDP aims to improve the job skills of black South Africans by reorganizing and greatly improving the educational system. Educational reform includes building new schools and ensuring that black teachers meet minimum teaching requirements.

Land redistribution and restitution is a big item on the RDP agenda. During apartheid the government seized the land owned by blacks and gave it to white farmers. By the time apartheid was dismantled, almost 80 percent of the country's land was in the hands of whites, who constituted only about 14 percent of the total population. The government hopes that in giving ancestral lands back to black families, it will provide blacks with the means to achieve equality with whites.

The plan has three parts. The first objective is to give land back to the original owners or to the heirs of the original owners. The second is to redistribute 30 percent of the country's farmland to the black majority. The third is to give black tenant farmers who have lived and worked at white farms for more than 20 years a chance to buy a respectable portion of the land. Many white commercial farmers, who are not faring well because of droughts and years of

Top: *International Committee of the Red Cross (ICRC) volunteers distribute food to residents in Bambayi township, near Durban.*
Bottom: *Peace Corps worker, John Keith, poses with new friends in South Africa. The Peace Corps' arrival in South Africa came three years after Mandela requested U.S. help in addressing his country's social and economic challenges.*

CICR/Luc Chessex

Photo courtesy of the Peace Corps

government assistance, are willing to sell, but other white farmers fear the new policy. In these cases, the government has compensated white farmers with payment or a new patch of land. Since the government started the program in 1995, however, less than 1 percent of the land has been returned to nonwhite claimants.

Some white farmers like Hendrick Kritzinger, an Afrikaner who grows apples and pears in Eastern Cape Province, have decided to do their part. In 1996 Kritzinger helped 134 of his 500 employees buy a nearby farm, urging them to take advantage of government subsidies. He agreed to manage the farm and to show the new landowners how to run the business. But he fears that the owners still do not understand the project and will be so eager to get cash from crop sales that they will neglect to reinvest what is necessary to sustain the farm. "In the past," Kritzinger said, "we spent so much time telling these people, 'Don't think—just work.' Now all of a sudden, we are saying, 'You've got to think, then act.' It is very difficult."

HELP FROM OTHER SOURCES

Some international organizations that condemned apartheid in the early years are still helping its victims. The ICRC remains active in the country, distributing blankets and food to refugees of the political war in KwaZulu-Natal. Amnesty International opened its first office in South Africa in 1996 and continues to monitor human rights abuses there. In the same year, they sent delegates to South Africa to investigate political killings in KwaZulu-Natal. Delegates expressed concern about police brutality toward perpetrators of political killings in the province.

Aid agencies new to South Africa are pitching in to help rebuild. In February 1997, the first group of U.S. Peace Corps volunteers arrived in South Africa. According to Earl Yates, the South African Peace Corps director, the agency will work with the South African Ministry of Education to help teachers improve teaching methods in rural areas. The agency also intends to cooperate with local authorities to improve health care, water, transportation, and housing in the mostly poor and black Northern Cape Province. Britt Nelson, a 23-year-old volunteer from Minnesota, told the *Minneapolis Star Tribune* why she was particularly excited about going to South Africa. "Of all the countries, South Africa is trying more than anyone to change and make a better place."⊕

Search for Common Ground

South Africa's national television corporation teamed up with Search for Common Ground, a U.S. organization, to produce a 26-part television series about conflict resolution in South Africa. The series was very popular with South African viewers. Search for Common Ground has approached 24 other countries about airing the show, and all are interested. By focusing media attention on the actions of peace organizations—rather than on the violence and destruction of guerrillas—Search for Common Ground hopes the project will provide a call to action to victims of ethnic conflicts around the world.

EPILOGUE*

As the South African government grapples with the housing shortage, the crime problem, and the income gap between whites and blacks, all South Africans look to the future. Nelson Mandela has announced that he will not run in the 1999 presidential elections, but he has chosen Thabo Mbeki, a strong ANC leader to succeed him as head of the ANC. Overwhelming support for the ANC in the 1994 elections, makes the ANC the party to beat in 1999.

The strongest threat to the ANC power base appears to be the alliance between two new political parties, the New Process Movement (NPM) and the National Consultative Forum (NCF). Roelf Meyer, a former National Party (NP) member, formed the New Process Movement on May 18, 1997. De Klerk had selected Meyer to head a task force in charge of redesigning the NP. Meyer believed the NP should instead completely disband and start from scratch. In late 1997, Meyer's New Process Movement joined ranks with the NCF, whose leader is Bantu Holomisa, a former prominent member of the ANC.

The NP continues its struggle to rebuild the party after de Klerk's retirement from the politics. Conservatives and moderates also remain divided about how the party should approach the 1999 elections.

Changes on the political front have sparked new rivalries. In October 1997, political violence erupted between members of the NCF and the ANC in Cape Town's black townships and near the town of Richmond in Eastern Cape Province. Both sides accused one another of foul play and intimidation.

Meanwhile, Truth and Reconciliation hearings are scheduled to end in December 1997, but a final report on the commission's findings is not expected before June 1998. Of the 6,000 to 7,000 applications the commission has received, it has made a decision on only 100 cases. Half were rejected, and the rest were granted amnesty.

*Please note: The information presented in *South Africa: Nation in Transition* was current at the time of the book's publication. For the most recent information about the conflict, look for articles in the international section of U.S. daily newspapers. *The Economist*, a weekly magazine, is also a good source for up-to-date information. You may wish to access, via the Internet, *Independent Online*, a source for news from all prominent South African newspapers: http://www.inc.co.za/online/news/. For other internet resources regarding South Africa, access Ananzi, the South Africa search engine at http://ananzi.co.za/ or Link 2 South Africa at http://www.link2southafrica.com. For information about the TRC hearings, try http://www.truth.org.za/.

CHRONOLOGY

ca. A.D. 1500   Khoisan and Bantu-speaking peoples established in present-day South Africa.

ca. 1590   The Cape of Good Hope becomes a stop for English and Dutch sailors on their way to Asia.

1652   Dutch East India Company establishes a settlement at the Cape of Good Hope, where sailors can rest, restock their food supply, and tend to the sick.

1659   Dutch attack Khoisan after disputes over land and cattle. Era of low-intensity warfare begins.

ca. 1690   Dutch import slaves to work their farms in the Cape. Flemish, Scandinavian, French, and German immigrants willing to grow food for the Dutch East India Company also settle in South Africa.

1770s   European farmers (known as Boers) travel north and east, away from the Cape and the influence of the Dutch East India Company. Adventurers encounter resistance from the Khoisan and the Xhosa when they try to seize land for farming.

1775   British take control of the Cape colony from the Dutch.

1807–13   British abolish the slave trade, upsetting the Boers, who rely on slave labor to run their farms.

1833   Britain abolishes slavery in all of its colonies, including the Cape.

1838   In what is called the Great Trek (Voortrek), thousands of Boers leave the Cape colony and British rule to go farther north and east, into Zulu chiefdoms. The Zulus fight the Boers for land, but the whites' superior weapons soon defeat them.

1854   The British accept the independence of two Boer republics, Transvaal and Orange Free State. Cape colony and Natal are in British hands.

1867–77   With the discovery of diamonds and gold in Transvaal, British adventurers flood into the area to seek their fortunes. British pass laws to annex the Transvaal, upsetting many Boers.

1895–1896   The Boers (Afrikaners) respond to the influx by heavily taxing British companies and by refusing to grant British miners equal status. British troops enter the area and try to overthrow the Transvaal government, but the Boers defeat them in what becomes known as the first Anglo-Boer war.

1899–1902   On October 11, 1899 the Boers declare war on Britain. After heavy fighting, the British defeat the Boers in 1902 in the second Anglo-Boer war.

1910   The British establish the Union of South Africa.

1912   Black leaders form the South African Native National Congress (SANNC) to promote black civil rights through nonviolent forms of protest (later African National Congress, ANC).

1913–27   The South African government passes laws to limit where nonwhites can live.

1939   World War II begins and South Africa joins the war on the Britain's side.

1948   Daniel F. Malan, an Afrikaner member of the all-white National Party, wins South Africa's presidential elections. Malan enacts apartheid, a program that guarantees whites advantages over blacks in every aspect of life.

1949   The Malan administration passes the Prohibition of Mixed Marriages and Immorality Act, the Group Areas Act, and the Population Registration Act. All black South Africans are required to carry identity passes (passbooks).

1950   The apartheid government passes the Suppression of Communism Act.

1952   ANC, South African Indian Congress (SAIC), and other anti-apartheid groups launch the Defiance Campaign. They stage nonviolent strikes, sit-ins, rallies, and marches.

1955   People from all ethnic backgrounds found the Congress of the People and write the Freedom Charter, which outlines a plan for a nonracial, democratic South Africa. Blacks are forced out of their homes in Sophiatown, a black suburb of Johannesburg. The government bulldozes the homes and moves blacks to homelands, areas set aside for nonwhites, often in remote areas of the country.

1956   Voting rights enjoyed since 1853 by Coloureds living in the Cape Province are repealed.

1958   New Nationalist president Hendrik Verwoerd strengthens apartheid policies.

1959   Parliament passes the Promotion of Bantu Self Government Act, granting homelands self-rule.

1960   In March police killed 69 blacks in Sharpeville, a black township near Johannesburg.

1962   The government passes the Sabotage Act, which enables police to immediately arrest Nelson Mandela, Walter Sisulu, and other high-ranking ANC leaders.

1964   Nelson Mandela and Walter Sisulu are sentenced to life imprisonment.

1967   The government bulldozes District 6, a Coloured area of Cape Town, and relocates the residents to the Cape Flats.

1976   Students in the black township of Soweto (located near Johannesburg) protest a new law requiring classes to be taught in Afrikaans. Police kill several students, igniting a series of nationwide riots. Steve Biko, a young black student activist, forms the Black Consciousness Movement.

1977   Steve Biko, arrested under the Sabotage Act, dies in police custody. Countries around the world begin to impose economic sanctions on South Africa.

1983   Blacks riot in Sharpeville over pass law arrests, trespassing arrests, and curfew offense arrests.

1984   To quell violence, newly elected Nationalist president P.W. Botha relaxes minor apartheid laws and grants voting rights to Coloureds and Asians. Violence in black neighborhoods escalates.

1986   The United States and Great Britain join other countries in opposing apartheid through economic sanctions, which begin to hurt the South African economy.

1989   Nationalist F.W. de Klerk becomes president of South Africa and announces plans to release Nelson Mandela, legalize all political opposition groups, and to dismantle apartheid.

1990   The government begins negotiations with the ANC and other opposition groups for the transition to majority rule.

1991   The multiparty Convention for a Democratic South Africa (CODESA) met for the first time in December to discuss transferring power to the black majority, but disagreements stall talks.

1993   Anti-Communist activists murder Chris Hani, leader of the ANC's military wing (Umkhonto we Sizwe, leading to an explosion of violence and anti-white sentiment in black neighborhoods.

1994   The first national nonracial election is held in April. Nelson Mandela becomes president of South Africa. The new government implements the Reconstruction and Development Program.

1995   Mandela establishes the Truth and Reconciliation Commission (TRC).

1997   De Klerk retires from politics to give the National Party a chance to prepare for the 1999 presidential elections. Nelson Mandela announces he will not seek re-election in 1999. He promotes his deputy president, Thabo Mbeki, as successor to the ANC presidency. Police who murdered Steve Biko in 1977 and anti-communist activists who killed Chris Hani testify before the TRC.

SELECTED BIBLIOGRAPHY

Books and Articles

De Gruchy, John W. "Sharpeville Revisited." *The Christian Century*, April 26, 1995 v112 n14 p447(1).

Gordon, Myles. "The Road to Freedom." *Scholastic Update*, Feb 25, 1994 v126 n10 p 16(5).

Lyman, Princeton N. "South Africa's Promise." *Foreign Policy*, Spring 1996 n102 p105(15).

Mattera, Don. *Sophiatown: Coming of Age in South Africa*. Boston: Beacon Press, 1987.

Meisel, Jacqueline Drobis. *South Africa at the Crossroads*. Brookfield, CT: Millbrook Press, 1994.

Meredith, Martin. *In the Name of Apartheid: South Africa in the Postwar Era*. New York: Harper & Row, 1988.

Mufson, Steven. *Fighting Years: Black Resistance and the Struggle for a New South Africa*. Boston: Beacon Press, 1990.

Munro, David, and Alan J. Day. *A World Record of Major Conflict Areas*. Chicago: St. James Press, 1990.

Nelson, Harold D. *South Africa: A Country Study*. Washington D.C.: Foreign Area Studies, the American University; Headquarters, Department of the Army, 1982.

Paton, Jonathan. *The Land and People of South Africa*. Philadelphia: J. P. Lippincott, 1990.

Reader's Digest Illustrated History of South Africa: The Real Story. Expanded 3rd ed. Cape Town, South Africa: Reader's Digest Association South Africa,1994.

Shillington, Kevin. *A History of Southern Africa*. Burnt Mill, Harlow, Essex, England : Longman, 1993, 1987.

"South Africa Rejoins the World Community; Nelson Mandela Elected President." UN Chronicle, Sept 1994 v31 n3 p4(5).

Thompson, Leonard. *A History of South Africa*, Revised ed. New Haven, CT: Yale University Press, 1995.

Thompson, Leonard. *The Political Mythology of Apartheid*. New Haven, CT: Yale University Press, 1985.

Watson, R.L. *South Africa in Pictures*. Minneapolis: Lerner Publications Company, 1996.

Videos

"Mandela: The Man and His Country." ABC News, 1990.

"7 up South Africa." Newton, N.J: Shanachie, 1993.

"Witness to Apartheid." S. Sopher, 1986. Distributed by Du Art Video.

INDEX

ABOUT THE AUTHOR

Peter Kizilos is an award-winning author and communications consultant who lives in Minneapolis, Minnesota. He has written articles for major state and national publications and several books, including *Miles to Go Before I Sleep: My Grateful Journey Back from the Hijacking of Egyptair Flight 648* with Jackie Nink Pflug. For his commitment to leadership in public affairs, Peter was named a Mondale Fellow by the University of Minnesota's Hubert H. Humphrey Institute of Public Affairs. Peter received his B.A., cum laude, from Yale University and an M.A. in area studies from the University of Michigan–Ann Arbor.

ABOUT THE CONSULTANTS

Andrew Bell-Fialkoff, *World in Conflict* series consultant, is a specialist on nationalism, ethnicity, and ethnic conflict. He is the author of *Ethnic Cleansing,* published by St. Martin's Press in 1996, and has written numerous articles for *Foreign Affairs* and other journals. He is currently writing a book on the role of migration in the history of the Eurasian Steppe. Bell-Fialkoff lives in Bradford, Massachusetts.

R. L. Watson is a professor of history at North Carolina Wesleyan College and holds a doctorate in African history from Boston University. He has written numerous articles on South African history and the book *The Slave Question: Liberty and Property in South Africa,* published in 1990. He also prepared *South Africa in Pictures,* published by Lerner Publications Company in 1988, updated in 1996.

SOURCES OF QUOTED MATERIAL

p. 23 Suzanne Daley, "South Africa Democracy Stumbles in Old Rivalry," *New York Times,* 7 January 1996, 7; p. 25 *The Star* [South Africa], 25 May 1997, Editorial Page; p. 29 "De Klerk's Party Says It's Leaving South Africa's Government of National Unity," *Minneapolis Star Tribune,* 10 May 1996, 7A; p. 53 "Cool Down and Take Your Things," *Reader's Digest Illustrated History of South Africa: The Real Story.* Expanded 3rd ed. Cape Town, South Africa (Reader's Digest Association South Africa, 1994), 427; p. 55 "No More Black South Africans," *Reader's Digest Illustrated History of South Africa: The Real Story.* Expanded 3rd ed. Cape Town, South Africa (Reader's Digest Association South Africa, 1994), 425; p. 56 *Manifesto of Umkhonto we Sizwe,* 16 December 1961, ANC Historical Documents Web Site, http://www.anc.org.za.ancdocs/history; p. 58 Eric Black, "A Country Embarks on a Road Not Traveled," *Minneapolis Star Tribune,* 24 April 1994, 7P; p. 59 Ken Wells, "Mixed Feelings: 'Coloreds' Struggle to Find Their Place In a Free South Africa," *The Wall Street Journal,* 6 December 1995, 1; p. 69 F.W. de Klerk, "Normalizing the Political Process in South Africa: The Time for Negotiation Has Arrived," *Vital Speeches,* v56 n10 (1 March 1990): 290(6); p. 80 Anthony Lewis, "The Mandela Behind the Saint," *New York Times Magazine,* 23 March 1997, 40; p. 81 (top of page) Suzanne Daley, "Zulu-Based Party Quits Talks in South Africa," *New York Times,* 9 August 1997, A5; p. 81 (bottom of page) Myles Gordon, "The Road to Freedom," *Scholastic Update* 126, no. 10 (25 February 1994): 16; p. 84 Frank Wright, "Despite Struggles, South Africa is Showing Progress," *Minneapolis Star Tribune,* 14 June 1997, A9; p. 85 Anton Ferreira, "Mandela's Old Jail Opened to Public," *Washington Post,* 2 January 1997, A12; p. 86 Anthony Lewis, "The Mandela Behind the Saint," *New York Times Magazine,* 23 March 1997, 54; p. 89 Suzanne Daley, "Afrikaner Farmer Decides to Make Up for the Evils of Apartheid," *Minneapolis Star Tribune,* 2 March 1997, A10; p. 89 Robert Franklin, "Lakeland Woman, Peace Corps Reaching Out to South Africa," *Minneapolis Star Tribune,* 2 February 1997, A1.